Everyone has a Story

VICKY BRESLIN

ISBN 978-1-957220-11-6 (paperback)
ISBN 978-1-957220-12-3 (hardcover)
ISBN 978-1-957220-13-0 (digital)

Rushmore Press LLC
1 800 460 9188
www.rushmorepress.com

Printed in the United States of America

CONTENTS

PROLOGUE

IMAGINE LIFE IN THE EARLY 1950s. Doctors smoked while they were examining you. Dentists gave you certificates for a free ice cream after your visit to their office. You played outdoors. I remember playing in the vacant lots in our neighborhoods. We knew where they all were, and there was nothing empty about them. Those were the places where imagination exploded. Everything was there, all the tools we needed to create everything we could conjure up. Dirt, grass, bugs, leaves, trees, branches, rocks and abandoned items and sometimes a small source of water. It was just an adventure waiting to happen.

There was nothing vacant about those lots. They were a canvas that was waiting to be created with a child's unfiltered desires of greatness. Whatever was going on at home was forgotten the moment your feet touched the soil of that vacant lot.

A friend of mine once told me that if you could roll the roof back of people's houses and look inside you might be very surprised as to what might be going on. Everything is not as it seems. This indeed was true in the fifties. It was certainly true in my house. People didn't talk about their feelings or show much affection. I love you was not three words I had ever heard from anyone in my family.

Our role models all smoked and drank liquor. The television came in black and white with three stations. Private telephone lines were for the wealthy. We had third party lines. The other people that shared the line could listen in to your conversation any time they wanted. Girls wore dresses to school and church. You ate dinner every night with your whole family. It was home-cooked by your mother. Of course, you were required to help with the preparation. Setting the table was an unspoken rule. There were keys left in the car when you parked it outside of your house. The door to your house was usually unlocked. A bicycle and walking were the typical way that you got around. Life was good for most. Birth control and abortions were not spoken about. Having a baby out of wedlock was unheard of. This was the time that I came into the world. I was born to a 16-year-old unwed teenager and an absentee father.

FOREWORD

THIS STORY IS ABOUT MY life as I have lived it. I never talked about my past very much, I felt very embarrassed about where I came from. I did not want anyone to judge me from my past. I wanted you to watch me now. Look at me and my actions that I have shown you. If you liked what you have experienced with me so far, follow along and be a part of my journey. I am not for everybody.

This is not a novel of flowery descriptions and hard to spell adjectives. It is very much like me, concise and to the point. I make no excuses for my family or how they interacted with me. My life as a child made me who I am today. I am proud of myself. Writing this book made it possible to really explore my deepest feelings, how they affected me, and how I have affected others. If you choose to read this book, we will both be affected. I hope that my story will help you define your story, see your value and make it worth living.

INTRODUCTION

THIS IS A BOOK WRITTEN about how I became who I have grown to be.

I experienced many trials and tribulations along the way. Through it all, I developed a passion for life and discovery. I was often asked why I turned out so good with the history of my background. My reply was always the same. I wanted to treat people the way I wanted to be treated, not the way I was treated. There were people that helped me along the way, and I want to repay the kindness.

The first fifteen years of my life was controlled by others. Thanks to the love from many and especially my boyfriend I found love. My life now belonged to me. It was up to me to decide how I was going to live it. I felt everything terrible had happened to me already. That part of my life was in the past.

I was in control of myself now. I chose to live each day with a smile on my face. My sad days were over. Nothing but sunshine on my horizon. I believed in myself and that is how I chose to see my future.

Just because there was a bend in the road does not mean the end of the road. Determination was my driving force. The Holy Spirit gave me wings to fly. Discovery was and still is my desire. I hope that you can learn from my past, present, and the future. I know I have touched many lives with my story. I hope you are the next one. Everything is meant to be. If you decide to read it, you were meant to be touched by it.

WORDS OF PRAISE

VICKY BRESLIN'S STORY IS NOT a self-help book. It is a triumph over self-book. One that readers, people like you and me, can learn the most profound of life lessons. "That which does not kill us, makes us stronger," from German Philosopher Friedrich Nietzsche revered quotation.

Her memoir of growing up in an alcohol and drug infused household, with a brilliant but tortured mother and multiple siblings in a Southern California Beach town in the 1950 and 1960's. It opens a window into the heart, soul and inexpressibly creative mind of its author: how she embraced the chaos of her dysfunctional family. She made order from a childhood motto that she adopted as her lifetime mantra. "One minute has just passed, did you use wisely all sixty seconds?"

From childhood backyard theatricals to earn pocket money, to the establishment of a creative scrapbooking company generating millions in sales. Helping thousands of people to learn to express their own creativity. Teaching them to tell their own stories. The author reminds us that it all starts with you and how you choose to use the limited time that is given to you on this earth. To be generous to others, productive and most of all true to yourself. Learn how to use this time wisely, read this book.

Honest, insightful, plain speaking truth.

Learn how to use your time wisely and then tell your story.

-Anne Coffelt

Read this book.

It was mid-afternoon in a tiny mountain town in Northern California. As I peered through the store window, my heart began to race. I could barely contain my excitement.

It was as if every fiber of my artistic being was energized as I stared with amazement.

I could not help but feel that I knew the creator of this soulful store. But, it was closed, on a Wednesday, in the middle of the day! Why? Who was denying me the pleasure of strolling through this delightful, eclectic sea of treasures?

The sign said please call for an appointment and so I did. I made an appointment for the next day with Miss Vicky to visit her store. We became dear friends at that moment.

That fateful visit to a crazy, creative little place called the Funny Pharm changed me forever. Talking about and reading Miss Vicky's journey changed me. The emotional evolution of a person with abusive parents can go south at any moment yet Miss Vicky summoned her courage, strength, intellect and artistic soul to persevere. Her gentle, caring nature is quite different than her matter of fact writing style. Her love for fellow humans and animals is truly genuine. Miss Vicky's insightful wisdom into the tortured souls of others is a true testament to her triumph over her own tortured childhood. I know because we share some of the same emotional scars.

Miss Vicky has delivered her craftiness in many ways throughout her life. Her love and devotion to her family was a driving force in her ability to create under the most trying of circumstances. Tenacity prevailed when she became one of the first pioneers in the crafting industry.

Quite the journey from making mud pies in the backyard to showcasing her products on QVC.

This book is so much more; it is an emotional stroll through decades of life-changing experiences, challenges adventure, hope and love.

-Sussy Flanigan

Captivating from the very first page to the last. It leaves me waiting and wanting for the next two books. I feel now I am a part of her amazing journey.

-Cindy Goldman

DEDICATION

THE DEDICATION OF THIS BOOK is to the people in my life that I have met along the way because they are the ones that this book is written about. I would like to also dedicate this book to every one of you that decide to read it. There would be no story without each one of you. Who you become depends on the story that you tell with your own life experience.

I believe in the philosophy that one minute has just passed. Did you use wisely, all sixty seconds?

It is important to realize how many things can be experienced in just one minute.

CHAPTER ONE

One Night Stand

My father was a dancer.

My mother was immediately attracted to his charismatic personality, talent, and charm.

My mother was 16 years old. My father was 19 years old. My mother was a drug addict. My father was a pill popper.

Neither of my parents told me this story... I picked up bits and pieces from my relatives.

My mother and father never married. My mother took responsibility for my care. I was a One Night Stand.

I have pictured their story in my mind over and over.

It goes something like this. My father was dancing at a nightclub. He was competing in a dancing competition. My mother was there with her other teenage friends. She liked his dancing, energy and charisma. They both noticed each other. After my father won the competition my mother went to congratulate him. He thanked her and gave her a quick kiss. When the event was over, he invited her out to his car. She said yes and off they went. He pulled the car over and slipped into the back seat where they proceeded to make me. They finished their encounter by him dropping her off at her home. They didn't think about ever seeing each other again. The stars must have been aligned just right that night. That is when I was conceived. I have never discovered the true story and I probably never will. This story seems to work in my mind, and it is the one I believe in. Everyone has a story and this one is mine.

CHAPTER TWO

A Family of Strong Women

WHEN MY GRANNY WAS JUST twelve years old, she went in for an operation. I am not sure what kind of an operation, but they accidentally damaged her hearing and she came out of the surgery deaf.

My Granny was brought up as a very devout Catholic woman. She studied and committed her life to being a nun in the early stages of her life. She fulfilled her dream and became a nun and was devoted to the lord. She met my grandfather and left the convent. Lucretia and Wallace Burton were married quickly and started their new life together.

Together over their short marriage they had four daughters. The girls were all named after strong women from the bible. My grandfather had an addiction to alcohol. His life was short, and he died a painful death from his alcoholism.

My Granny was deaf, widowed and managed to raise four girls in Long Beach, California. It was in a low-income temporary housing project where they all five lived in a tent. In order to support her and her four children, she made a living mending silk stockings.

She was a very strict mother.

Because she could not hear, she made her own assumptions about how her children were behaving. She would punish them fiercely and physically. I am pretty sure this may have had a significant impact on my mother's behavior. I have always admired the courage and strength she must have had to accomplish raising her family. This was not an easy time but she persevered. I never once heard her complain about it.

I come from strong women which can be a curse and a blessing. I chose to make mine a blessing.

CHAPTER THREE

And so, the story goes...

So much of this information was told to me by my stepfather. When I would question him about why my mother was so mean and abusive.

From what he had been told, my granny was not a loving mother. She was harsh and took the bible very seriously. She was angry that she had left the church to be a wife and mother only to be left a widow. Raising four children by herself was no small task.

I have to say I felt so much admiration for her. She was always kind to me. I loved her profusely. I often felt very protective of her because of her not being able to hear. I felt I could be her ears. I got a spelling toy and I would talk to her with it.

I learned at a very young age how important communication is. I learned to be a very good communicator by overcoming obstacles.

CHAPTER FOUR

My Mother Was Always On The Move

My mom was the youngest child in the family, the baby.

From as far back as I could remember my mother acted very strange and erratic. A beer for breakfast and vodka all afternoon until the day was over. She loved to take speed (cross tops, whites was the name in the 60's) smoke marijuana and was a heroin addict when she got pregnant with me.

My mother used to tell me how I was the one that ruined her life. She made it clear I was unwanted and she would be happier without me.

She had tried to miscarry me and wanted to give me up for adoption.

I would wonder why none of her attempts had come to fruition. I often daydreamed about the nice family that would have adopted me. Wishing I could be living with them instead of my mother.

Since she was stuck with me, she would just drop me off at my grandmother or one of my aunt's homes. She would convince them that she would be right back. Sometimes it took her two years to get right back. So, I became very adaptable to different environments early on. I learned how to be able to move in an instant and enjoy wherever it was that I landed. I am pretty sure that anywhere I was living was better than living with her.

I decided to always see the good in my environment. I knew I wouldn't be there for very long.

CHAPTER FIVE

The Magical Bus Ride

I WAS VERY CLOSE TO my Granny as I called her. I stayed with her a lot of the time. She taught me about God, praying and how to be obedient. One time when I was four to five years old, we took a trip back East on the Greyhound Bus. Because she was deaf, I was her ears and tried to make sure everything went smoothly. I was always making sure she was never taken advantage of.

While we were traveling on the bus, we stopped in Las Vegas where I encountered my first slot machine. I will never forget the sounds of those slot machines. I was so thrilled to hear the coins come out of this shiny money spitting machine. The sound they made when the coins would fall into that silver tray. If you had won a lot, they would also fall out of the tray. I would chase them down to give to my Granny. It was thrilling. She used one of her nickels to give me a ride on one of the coin-operated kiddie rides at the next place that we stopped inside the bus station. I think the fact that the coin was from the slot machine made the ride so much more magical to me. While riding on the mechanical horse I had visions of galloping back to Las Vegas and gathering more coins. It was something I would always remember about that very long trip. In my way of thinking those nickels were free which made spending them so much sweeter.

It took several days to travel across the country on the bus. The biggest thrill for me about the bus was that it had a bathroom on it.

I loved using it, just knowing that we were driving down the road while I was using the bathroom. I imagined what everyone in their cars was thinking about as they drove past our bus without having their very own bathroom. It seemed like this is how a princess might live. Surely, they were envious of this deluxe mode of transportation. Surely, they wished they had a bathroom in their cars.

My mother had bought me cards that you could embroider on with yarn and a magnetic board game called wooly willy. I remember them being wrapped up and I was not to open them until I got on the bus. This is the first time I remember receiving a gift from her. I just knew this was how rich people traveled. You get presents on the bus, have your own toilet, go to exotic places like Las Vegas, get golden coins to take a ride and get to spend time with your favorite Granny. My imagination kept me entertained on the excursion. The excitement of what might happen next was just too much! How did I get so lucky to be on this magical bus ride?

I went on this trip on the presumption I would be helping my Granny and showing her how competent I was. It turned out that I had the best time of my life. She had helped me see all kinds of new things. She was the one who helped me.

CHAPTER SIX

Next Stop Ohio

WE GOT TO OUR DESTINATION and stayed with Granny's sister, my great aunt, great uncle and cousins. It was the first time I had met them. I had never seen snow. This just kept getting better and better.

The cousins were teenagers, and they decided to take me to the malt shop with them. I did not know what a malt shop was, but they told me it involved ice cream. I just couldn't get there quickly enough. They would drop their coins into this amazing machine with records in it. It had neon lights and sounds came out of it. It was called a jukebox. I had never seen one, but I knew I loved it. We would then listen to Elvis singing Love me Tender on this jukebox. They would giggle and act all twitterpated. They wore poodle skirts, cashmere sweaters, and ponytails. Watching all of this made me forget why we were here. It was for the ice cream. We sat down in a booth and ordered our ice cream. I licked every drop of my dessert while listening to the jukebox and just watching these cousins that were a part of my family. I loved being around them and thought they were terrific! I was in awe. Could this top the bus ride and chasing the coins in Las Vegas?

We made a snowman and had big family dinners. I wanted to stay there forever.

We stayed for quite a while before venturing back to California. I remember it as one of the happiest times of my young life. I felt a sense of family and that I was proud to be a part of it. Looking back now I realize what a magical time it was to be a part of their Elvis experience too. It was great being included in an ordinary family. I was too young to appreciate Elvis, but I knew he must have been something special.

This trip helped me to see that not all families are mean and hurtful. Some people are pretty darn nice. I had nice family members, I just didn't live with them. You cannot choose your family but you certainly can choose the people you want to spend your time with.

CHAPTER SEVEN

Time To Be Moving On

I CRIED A MILLION TEARS when it was time to leave. The only positive was that I got to get back on that bus with the toilet.

When we returned, my mother was living with a new man. I am not sure if they were married at the time. But I settled into living in a new home with two parents. This was a brand-new experience for me. I had never lived with a man before. I thought that this man was my father. He seemed to like me and I sure took a liking to him. I used to get up in his lap and he made me feel safe. He had been in the military and had some hula girl tattoos. He used to make them dance by flexing his muscles. I loved that.

We lived in Lakeport, California, and I now had a dog named tag. I used to catch frogs, and we would eat their legs. We had chickens. They harvested them, and my mother liked me to scratch her back with the cut off chicken feet that had long claws. I remember feeling special that she wanted me to do it. It was the only time I could remember her ever having physical contact with me. I had a lamb, and I used to feed it with a baby bottle. My new dad loved to fish, and I would get to go to the lake with him. I remember getting caught up in the fishing line when he cast his line into the water one time. He was mad, I cried. I did not get invited on too many more fishing trips to the lake after that. He had warned me several times not to get in his way when he was throwing out the line. I got distracted and ignored him. I loved living there. I remember a large hill in our backyard. I would put the hose at the top of the hill and turn the water on. It made it real muddy. Perfect for sliding on it all the way to the bottom. I would hose myself off before going in the house to take a bath. I spent most of the time outdoors and wandering around exploring with my dog Tag. I remember we used to go to a roller skating rink there. That is where I learned how to roller skate.

I never knew why but we moved out in the middle of the night. They made a nice little bed for me in the back-seat window of our car. The only thing we took with us was the things that fit in the car. Everything was gone as quickly as it appeared. No more lamb, frogs, chickens or my dog Tag. Poof like they never existed. They were all gone and never to be spoken of again. We never went back to Lakeport but I never forgot the good times I had there.

I often didn't know how things happened. I learned it really had nothing to do with me. I was just a passenger in someone else's story. All along creating my own story.

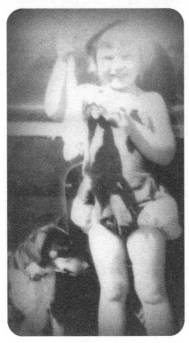

CHAPTER EIGHT

Making New Friends

WE MOVED TO LONG BEACH California. We moved into a new house. I longed for some pets. I got a chameleon lizard. I used to take it with me wherever I would go. I tied a ribbon to his neck like a little leash and I would keep him on my shoulder. I used to get up early in the morning and go visiting with one of our neighbors. She lived in an upstairs apartment, and she was elderly. We would have tea every morning. We would have long conversations. She lived alone and loved telling me stories. I would thank her for the tea and then sneak back into my house and go back to my room. I would get under the covers and wait for my mom to tell me it was time to get up.

One day the elderly woman met my mother and told her how much she enjoyed our morning visits. She thought I was a delightful child and was so happy to always have our early morning cups of tea. She appreciated my company.

My mom was so mad at me. I got a spanking like I will always remember. She had no idea what I had been doing every morning before she woke up. I think she must have been embarrassed that she had no idea I was out wandering around. I was then locked in my room at night. I cried and begged her not to close the door. I was afraid of the dark. I used to think she would somehow forget about me and leave me locked in there. To this day I cannot sleep or be in a room with a closed door.

I have recognized that I have certain feelings about things. It helps me to understand why I feel these ways. It is as if I can look at these things with wiser eyes and chase the thoughts away.

CHAPTER NINE

I Peed My Pants

I NEVER GOT TO SAY goodbye to my upstairs neighbor. I missed her a lot. I can't even remember her name and that makes me sad. I do have a picture of her and I and that makes me happy.

We soon moved after that, and I remember that I loved playing outside in the new neighborhood. I hated to be in the house. I never wanted to stop what I was doing outside so I would pee my pants rather than go inside. I would then get in big trouble for that. I got spanked and put in a corner for long periods of time. I never could figure out how she knew that I had peed my pants. By the time I had gotten in the house my pants were dry. Of course I would always lie and say I hadn't peed my pants. I asked her how she knew. She told me to look at my legs. They were always covered in dirt except where the pee had run down my legs. It made her mad that I had to put clean clothes on and take a bath. That was extra work for her. After that she would holler out the door to me while I would by playing with my friends. Vicky Lynn get in here and go to the bathroom so you don't pee your pants. The kids would look at me and ask why I peed my pants. I would always make up some magical story about it and run into the house. I soon hated going outside. Of course everyone would make fun of me and call me a baby. It wasn't long after that it was time to move again. I wasn't sad about leaving. My chameleon had gotten loose and I couldn't find him anywhere. I finally found him behind the couch all shrivelled up and dead. This made me sad and I was happy to find new friends that would not make fun of me.

I really thought about wetting the bed and peeing my pants a lot. Let's face it, that is not normal. I think it had to do with control. That was something I could control. I chose to conscientiously do it because I could. There was always the risk of being caught. But it was my choice to do so.

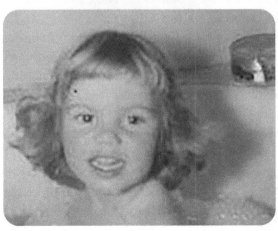

CHAPTER TEN

Christmas is Coming

OUR NEW HOME WAS NESTLED in a small oil town called Signal Hill. I was fascinated by the oil derricks pumping up and down. They reminded me of rocking horses. My parents had bought the house. It was the first time we actually were putting down roots. I was six years old and just starting kindergarten and Signal Hill elementary school.

Everything changed for me when we moved into this new house. My days as an only child was about to end abruptly. My mother was pregnant. I was so excited. In my mind it was like I was about to get my own living doll to play with. I had imagined all of the things that we would do as soon as the baby came home.

On Christmas Eve I was told to pack a bag, and I was going to go stay with my auntie Bert. My mother was having the baby. I was not happy about having to leave my house. What about Christmas, the presents? Would Santa know where to bring my gifts? I quickly snapped out of it and then I realized I would be getting the most amazing gift of all a new baby sister. My mind suddenly forgot all about Christmas. I imagined myself being a part of the celebration of the sweet baby Jesus being born. Wow I was getting a baby just like Mary and Joseph did on Christmas Eve. I was the luckiest person alive. I told my mom that the baby must be named Mary after the Virgin Mary.

My sister was born. I thought she would want to start playing with me right away. First things first: We would recreate the manger, and await the three wise men. Arriving by camels and donkeys they would bring their finest gifts. We may even have an angel or two, lamb, camel and a donkey show up. This was going to be the best Christmas ever.

Reality had set in. I had competition. She couldn't play with me. She cried all the time. There wasn't a single animal that showed up. Not one single angel. The only gifts were ones that were for her. This was not what I was looking forward to. Suddenly my dad acted like she was the only child in the house. What was I thinking? The worst Christmas of my life. It seemed as if no one cared about me. Everything changed for me and I wasn't sure where I stood.

I realized sometimes things don't turn out like I thought they would. But I never gave up hoping. Hoping and dreaming are sometimes way better than the reality that comes to fruition. I began to embrace dreaming. Dreaming is good.

CHAPTER 11

For the Love of Teaching and Learning Lessons

AS TIME WENT ON AND my sister got older I loved to teach her everything. One Christmas she received 19 dolls and a big toy box to put them all in. It had a chalkboard on the front of it, and it was perfect for playing school. I was not getting the attention, gifts and the love that my sister was and believe me I noticed it.

My Granny would come over and take me home with her on the bus. There was not a toilet on this small bus but the ride was short. When I would get there she had presents for me. We loved walking to the Recreation Park. We would sometimes go to the Pike and play Skee Ball. I would win a little plastic Cupie Doll. When my Mom would come to pick me up, I was not allowed to keep the gifts. She proclaimed that there would be gifts for both of us or none for me. I was so sad. I had seen my sister getting lots of presents, and I wasn't getting any. It really did not make any sense to me. I can clearly remember a fashion doll that I loved the most, but I could not have it. I dream of those cupie dolls. To this day I still want a Cupie Doll from the Pike.

My brother came shortly after. My Mom loved my brother so much and called him cuddles. She loved cuddling with him. I was happy for him, but I had never experienced any of that affection. In fact, my mom never once told me that she loved me my entire

35

life. It seemed strange to me that my dad adored my sister and my mom adored my brother. I felt like I was not really a part of the family.

When I was enrolled at Elementary School, I had a new last name. I had the same name as my siblings. I knew for sure this man was my Dad. He treated me very well. Nothing was ever said otherwise. One day when I was about 7 years old, my Mom told me to go get cleaned up and put on a dress. I obeyed, and a man came to the door. My Mom called me and said I was going with this man. We drove to a hospital. I remember he was tall and thin. He was kind of funny too. We went inside the hospital and visited with an elderly woman. I remember she had the most beautiful head of white hair. It was long, braided and placed in a crown upon her head. I thought she must be some sort of Queen like person. She seemed to shine like gold. She looked at the man I was with and said "I can go now. I have seen my son with his daughter." I turned around to see who she was talking about, but there was no one there. I remember feeling very strange about being there. I wondered if she had seen a ghost. She told me to give her a hug and a kiss. I very shyly approached her and complied. We left the hospital and the man took me home. I got out of the car and said goodbye. I ran into my house and nothing else was ever said about it to me.

Go with the flow was and will continue to always be my motto. Live in the moment and get whatever you can out of every minute of your life.

CHAPTER 12

I Begin To See The Light

THERE WAS A CITY COUNCIL meeting one night in our small town. My Mom brought me with her to it. She had been drinking and started ranting and raving. I remember sitting there and hearing people whispering, "Get her out of here." My first time I really remember being so embarrassed. I didn't know better and thought every family had these outbursts. It was the first time I realized this was a very dysfunctional family. This was only the beginning of many of my firsts!

Things started getting hectic in the home now. All of a sudden I found out my Dad had three sons by his first wife. It sort of made sense why he was so excited to have a baby girl. Her name was Dot and she and the three boys had come to stay with us. She had sat under a sunlamp and fallen asleep. The sunlamp fried her face. We had to care for her and the three boys. She was there for about six months. I liked having her there. She seemed very glamorous to me. She wore bright red lipstick and smoked her cigarettes with a very long cigarette holder. She always wore a tight fitting dress and high heels. She often wore hats. She was always kind to me and wore perfume. After she healed, she moved out, but the boys stayed. Having the new additions was fun. They were older, and I learned a lot from them.

I can remember one morning very vividly when my new brother made us pancakes for breakfast. Being the creative soul that he was he put some blue food coloring in the batter. I had never had blue pancakes. I couldn't wait to see what blue pancakes would taste like. I was thinking of the possibilities of all the colors that were possible. We could make purple ones by adding a little red to the batter. My mind was reeling. My sister was not happy with the change of color of her breakfast pancakes. She complained to my Mom, she was not going to eat blue pancakes.

My mom was a frugal person and she did not like any waste of food. This prompted my mother to call my Dad and relay the drama. He stopped what he was doing. He drove home from work and threw the pancake batter in my brother's face and proceeded to beat him. I was mortified and very scared. I felt so sorry for my brother. I helped him clean up the kitchen and told him I really liked the blue pancakes. His name was Johnny and I loved his creative soul.

His oldest son George, moved out right away after that. His youngest son, Danny, was put in a naval academy. I was so sad to have them gone. I really got used to having them around. My Dad continued giving Johnny beatings. I really was confused by this. Finally, his middle son left too. I remember crying when he told me was leaving. I enjoyed how he would play dolls with me and dress up. I later figured out that he was gay. My Dad was very macho. I think looking back that he was trying to beat it out of him. My Dad was starting to use speed around that time and I think it heightened his temper. His three boys died this way: George the Oldest died from complications of being an alcoholic. Johnny his middle son, died of suicide not long after he moved out of our home. I am certain it had to be from the rejection of his dad. His youngest expired in prison. He became a white power inmate. Someone disagreed with him and he was killed. I have always been sad for all of them. They all had great qualities in my eyes.

Different kinds of people came in and out of my life. I have always been excited to learn about them. What made them tick. How they were different from me. I am inquisitive about everyone I meet. I am always interested in hearing their story.

G-E Sunlamp tans like the sun, costs only $9⁹⁵

CHAPTER 13

Drugging, Drinking and Driving

My parents were heavy into drinking and drugging by this time. My Dad used to drive Jalopy Race Cars. He had his own auto repair business. He worked long hours. He liked to drink. With the mixture of the speed and the alcohol, he became very violent. This was not a good combination for him.

My Mother used to get bottles of Bubble Up and fill half of them up with vodka, half with bubble up and then recap them. You could not smell the alcohol on her breath. She started drinking all the time and she hid the bottles of liquor in the garage. She would have me get the bottle from the fridge and open it in front of everyone. She then made me take a drink and not make a face so that everyone thought it was just Bubble Up. I hated doing it, especially in front of my Granny. Everyone knew not to touch my mom's Bubble Up.

My Mom used to go South of the border into Mexico and bring back large bottles of speed. My job was to take 12 pills and roll them in aluminum foil into a sweet little package. She would then hide them. A red-headed man named Rusty would come by and pick them up. Sometimes a man named Joe would come with Rusty. They always reminded me of Abbott and Costello because they were so funny together. I learned later that he was a drug dealer selling them. My Dad was one of his customers. My Dad never knew my Mom was his supplier, or that I was the one who did the packaging. I was very proud of how quick I was and how good the rolls of speed looked. I never knew what it was or what I was involved in. One day I went with Joe on an errand to pick up something at the pharmacy for my mom. I remember Joe sticking a bottle of something down his pants and stealing it. I asked him why he did that and was promptly told to mind my own business. It was almost like stealing was an acceptable thing to do.

Lots of fighting, lots of beatings started being normal behavior in our home. One of my cousins, Diane, came to live with us around this time. She was near my Mother's age, and they started to party together. I became the house cleaner and babysitter. They became reckless and irresponsible.

I was good at helping my mom hide her addictions. I never liked the behavior and swore to myself I would never be like her.

CHAPTER 14

Me and My Big Mouth

Even at my young age, I felt our family was seriously spinning out of control. One morning my Dad announced he was going to the market. I asked if I could ride along with him. I could always talk him into getting me a treat. We did our shopping, and he told me to wait in the car. I did as he said, but I kept a watchful eye on him. He ducked into a phone booth and made a quick call. We then made our way back home. I innocently told my Mom that while we were at the market, my Dad had used the phone booth. We sat down to eat our meal.

The next thing I knew my dad picked up his glass of milk and threw it at my face. I was so surprised and hurt. I started out having such a great day. What happened? I got up from the table crying to go clean up and change my clothes. My Dad vacated the table too. He got in his car and drove off. I was so confused. My Dad vacated the table too. He got in his car and drove off. I was so confused. It wasn't until years later that I learned that I had exposed his cheating with another woman. He was cheating on my Mom. My Mom was drinking more than ever. She tried to commit suicide. I was awakened by a very nice police officer telling me that he was taking my Mom to the hospital. My Dad was with his girlfriend. He asked if I would be able to watch the kids. I said yes. I didn't realize what she had done until much later. What do you do after that? You have another baby of course. So stupid! My parents were not living with each other at this time. He was living with his new girlfriend. Her name was Patty, and we were all instructed to call her the creature. My Mom decided to make it her life's mission to make the creature and my Dad miserable. She found out where the creature lived, and we would all pile in the car. Nightly drives were made to harass them. I hated it, and I was so embarrassed. I felt so bad for my dad and his lover. He returned to our home.

This turn of events really changed our family forever. I realized I had started it by innocently disclosing the phone booth call. I started getting a lot of spankings with the belt from my dad after that. One night after being gone with my mom all day, we pulled into the driveway. I saw all these broken bottles of liquor. My dad had found her hiding places and smashed all of it. When we went into the house, I was sent to my room immediately. That was the first time I had ever heard my dad cry. He said he just couldn't take it anymore. He gave her a beating. She was bleeding. She decided to go out that night. I remember when she left, he said: "Have a ball, have two of them." I did not know what that meant but I was sure of one thing, I was glad she got the beating. I told my sister that I thought she deserved it. I was devastated that she had made my dad cry. I hated her drinking as much as he did. My sister told my mom what I had said. I got a massive beating for that. She said I deserved it. I believed I did.

I believed I deserved a lot of bad things. But I always wondered why I was not worthy of love. I would try so hard to be perfect. I was never good enough for them. I felt I was good enough for me and that was just going to have to be good enough.

things fall apart so
that other things
can fall together

CHAPTER 15

A Change Was Coming

EVERY MORNING IN THE SUMMER my mom would take us to the thrift stores. We would run around the store like crazy kids and pick out things we wanted. We usually got to pick one thing to take home. I shared my room with my sister. We had shelves on all the walls. They were full of stuff from the thrift stores. I was always a very organized person my sister was not. I put a piece of string down the middle of the room. I kept my side neat and tidy. She kept hers a mess. That all changed one day when my dad came home drunk. He had decided he did not like all the stuff on the shelves. He came into the room and smashed everything and tore the string down. I was told to clean it all up and throw it all away. He ordered my mom out of the house. I ran out and hid in the car. He found me there and dragged me back into the house and gave me a colossal spanking. It became clear to me later what this was all about. My mom and dad were going to be splitting up soon. I don't think anyone knew it, but I felt it.

I spent a tremendous amount of time when I was young playing with Barbie Dolls. I was obsessed with them. My mom would pick up stuff at the thrift stores and make the most beautiful outfits for my dolls. She had worked at Mattel when I was young, I thought that was so cool. I used to build the best doll houses out of cardboard boxes. I made curtains, rugs, and chandeliers. I would use 45's on my record player and play songs like "get out in that kitchen and rattle those pots and pans." I would have Ken saying that to Barbie. I loved finding just the right songs for the perfect words to play and pretend they were saying them to each other. Ken and Barbie would then act out what they had just sung to each other. I would decorate the house with matching everything. What I didn't have I would cut out the pictures from the Big Sears Department Store catalog. I got a ton of ideas from that publication.

If it was light out, we were to play outside. If it was dark, we were to be in our rooms. We were not allowed to watch TV. We had a big backyard. There was a little rental home in the back also. A plethora of new folks moving in and out. There was a mature persimmon tree, two avocado trees, a lemon tree, and a vegetable garden. These trees shed a ton of leaves. There was a lot of raking to do. I was usually the one who did the raking. When the persimmons were not fully ripe, they would make your whole face pucker. I loved having the neighborhood kids come over, and I would talk them into trying my persimmons (unripe of course). Their faces would start to make funny faces, and I would laugh so hard. It became an initiation into my backyard of creativity. Our laundry room was outside in a little building. My mom kept her big box of laundry soap in there. One time I made a bunch of mud balls. I then rolled them into the white detergent and stacked them up. I remembered how fun it was to make snowballs that I had learned to make from my trip back East with my granny. I made tacos out of the persimmon leaves. I folded them in half, put mud in the middle and then freshly picked grass for the cheese. I invited the neighborhood kids over for tacos and a snowball fight. When my mom went to do the laundry, she found traces of mud in the detergent. She asked me about it, and of course, I got in big trouble. I was wasting detergent and that cost her money. But it was so worth it.

I loved organizing and preparing for fun events. It kept me busy and I was good at it.

CHAPTER 16

Entrepreneur In Training

I STARTED WORKING WHEN I turned about 10 years old. It took my mind off my family's downward spiral. Backyard shows were like a full-time job. I would work on coordinating and organizing different events all the time. I liked doing circus shows, talent shows, little art galleries, fashion shows, music, and dance shows. The record player was a big part of all my shows. My mom would buy me the supplies to make ice cream sundaes. I would sell them at the events. She made me pay her for the cost of the goods, and I got to keep the rest. There was always a friendly crowd. I charged admission and sold the sundaes that I had made for. I watered and raked my neighbor's yards for a quarter. One of my neighbors raised pheasants and birds. I would help her feed them and clean up after them. The birds were so much fun to watch over. They were beautiful. I loved watching the little chicks hatch in the incubator and I would name each one of them. It gave me a little spending money for the thrift stores.

Babysitting was an excellent source of income. I used to watch the cutest little girl named Edwina. The only thing I knew about babysitting was from my personal experiences. Her mother was a nurse working the night shift. I would come at night and stay until the morning. As part of our nightly rituals in my family, we would eat dinner, take a bath and wash our hair followed the same course. I followed the course with Edwina. I gave her an evening meal, told her to brush her teeth, gave her a bath, and began shampooing her hair. She complied readily with all my requests until it came to the washing of her hair. She said her Momma would be mad if she shampooed her hair. I told her not to worry; I would take responsibility for it. I began taking her barrettes out and removing her braids and finally the rubber bands. As soon as I put the water & shampoo on her head, it started expanding like a pop-up sponge. It took on the coarseness of a Brillo Pad. I could not get it back into its beautiful shiny state that it was in before I washed it. She said her momma was going to kill me. Well, when her mama got home, and she woke Edwina up to get ready for school...she was so angry. I told her what happened, and she said it would take her hours to get her hair ready. That is when I realized that black people and white people had different kinds of hair. I never asked her to wash her hair as part of the bedtime routine again.

I watched another little boy from the neighborhood. His mother did not tell me that he liked to crawl out of his bedroom window and go wandering. I did the nightly rituals. Tucked him in, told him a story and said the nightly prayers. I went in about an hour later to check on him, and he was gone. I panicked. I looked everywhere for him. Inside the house, outside the house and up and down the block. When I got back to the house, he was back in his bed. When I went home that night, I looked up his name in my book of names and their meanings. His name meant wanderer, enough said.

I decided putting on the talent shows was a much more fun and a less stressful way to earn some cash!

We lived two doors down from a convalescent home. There was the sweetest lady who lived next door. She could not get around very well. She was a widow. I used to go over and water and rake up the leaves from her large fig tree. She would reward me with a bit of cash and orange cookies with cream cheese frosting. I searched my whole life for that recipe. I never could find it. I have never forgotten the longing for one more taste of those cookies. Sadly, one day she passed away. I lost an excellent source of income, my favorite cookies, and a wonderful friend.

Hard work, being dependable and a hunger for cash gave me the drive to make money. And let's just say I was hungry.

CHAPTER 17

The Summer of 1964

MY FAVORITE NEIGHBOR'S HOUSE WAS bought by the hospital to expand its facility. They demolished it. We had the pleasure of a vacant lot next door to our home. I went straight to work to start building myself a pool. I gathered as many volunteers as I could to help me to begin digging. We dreamed of having a beautiful swimming pool. From the moment I woke up until I had to be called in, I would be outside digging my future pool. I would work on that pool all summer long. I finally got something deep and wide enough that I felt we could splash around in. I decided to go ahead and fill it up with water and reap my rewards. I had no idea that all I was really doing was making a huge mud bath. I got it filled up to the top. My sister came outside to let me know it was time to get cleaned up because we were going to go out to dinner. I turned the hose off and went inside to get ready. When it was time to get into the car to leave my Dad called for my sister. She could not be found in the house. I heard her cry out, "I'm in the pool." In amazement, I jumped out of the car and ran to my pool. How dare she be the first one in. She had climbed into it with all her fancy clothes and shoes on. It kind of ruined the evening and we did not go out to dinner. Once again it was time for a good spanking. Yes, indeed my Dad was so mad. He was not aware of my building of the pool. The next day was spent filling the pool in with dirt. I never even thought that cement might be needed to make that pool something to swim in. Not to mention, it was not our property. Lesson learned! I still want a pool in my yard and I love to swim. I actually like to get a mud bath at the spa too. Before you dive into a project though I learned to look before you leaped.

CHAPTER 18

My Life Of Fantasy Playing

As I AM GROWING OLDER I still really love to play. Here are just a few of my favorite childhood play days.

Another fun thing about living near the hospital was that I used to walk by the hospital windows on my way to school. I used to wave to all the people inside. As I got older, I would go inside and visit with them. I would take the flowers that I had picked and told them stories. Once again, I had forgotten to mention this to my mom. One day, the hospital came over and brought me an old wheelchair that they could no longer use. They told my mom how much joy I had brought the folks when I visited them. They knew I would just find the perfect use for this old chair. A spanking was given for not telling anyone that I had been going in there. Apparently I needed permission which I did not ask for. SO MANY RULES The wheelchair remained, and we played in that thing for so many years. All the kids in the neighborhood would come to play in it. I even used to make fake casts and made a pretend hospital. I, of course, was the head nurse. I would never dream of being a doctor. I would pick up all kinds of medical supplies at the Salvation Army. Candy pills medicine in plastic prescription bottles with labels was prevalent and easily dispensed. I had started an administration office that you needed to go to before you got to see the nurse. I would go to the bank with my Mom and pick up deposit and withdrawal slips. I picked up some used rubber stamps, rubber bands, stapler, hole punch, forms and stamp pad at the thrift store and set up my office. I even had a rolodex with all the medical information you could imagine. I made fake bandages and splints. There was usually a head bandage too.

I do believe that my generation was the last one that really played outdoors. I felt so lucky to have my birthday in the summertime. For my birthday I got things like slip and slide, slinky, pogo stick, Eskimo yo-yo, water wiggle, pick up sticks, jacks, marbles, BARBIE, Lincoln logs, Mr. Machine, play dough, monopoly, game of LIFE, Mr. Potato head, etch a sketch, roller skates with a key, jump rope, Chinese jump rope, kites, carrom board, checkers, dominoes, silly putty, color forms, Lite Brite, musical bells, xylophone, and water toys. Just to name a few that I can remember. Cardboard boxes were one of my favorite items to create with. I made train cars out of the bigger boxes. I put a hole in the side and strung a piece of rope through it. My friends could get inside and hold onto the line. The other end was tied to my bicycle, and I would give you a ride on my train. I had an engineer hat and a train whistle that I had gotten at the thrift store. I made little tickets, and I would punch them with my hole punch. All Aboard! I remember lots of stubbed toes as I never wore shoes. I loved being the train conductor.

Beauty Pageants were one of my favorite activities. I stopped doing the pageants after I didn't get crowned the winner once. It really wasn't fun for me to be the loser. I wanted to win! Being a Queen for a day was popular at that time. I fantasized about winning that title quite a lot. I put on my own shows. I would crown myself with a tiara made from construction paper. Wrapped boxes with nothing in them were the gifts. It did not matter that they were empty because they looked fabulous. I made big bows and used colorful tags. I would write on them, "you are a queen for the day!" I believed I could be Queen For The Day every day! All I needed was a sash to announce to the world I was a winner.

The gift of the outdoors, living in Southern California in the 1950s and 1960s was the best gift I could have ever been given. My birthday celebrated Summer. I loved that celebration every day. Waking up in the morning was such a joy because I could get outdoors. Anything to escape what was going on inside. I still love the sunshine and water that I was exposed to as a child. The beach is where I am the most comfortable. The salt air wraps around my body like a soothing lotion.

Being resourceful has always been one of my attributes. Making do with what I had. There was nothing wrong with that. I was amazed at what I could come up with. Determination to get whatever I thought I needed was always on my mind. I looked at everything with it's potential in my mind.

CHAPTER 19

School Is Home

GOING TO SCHOOL WAS SUCH a great place for me. I loved everything about it. Recess was the best part of the day. Tetherball, the rings, dodgeball, the bars, and hopscotch. I was like a sponge. So many exciting things to learn. My teachers were nice. I got my own desk, and I filled it with school supplies. Pencils, erasers and lined paper were some of my treasures. I loved keeping my school desk clean and organized. Learning came quickly to me. When I would get homework, I couldn't wait to get it done. When it was time to go home, I would be sad.

When I would walk into the house after school, the first thing I would do was sniff the air inside. I could smell the liquor, cigarettes, and drugs. Depending on how strong the smell was determined the chaos I was walking into. Recently I looked at my report cards from Elementary School. I had 22 absences and 10 tardies in one quarter. My mom preferred me to be home. It was a lot of work for her to get up and get me ready to go to school. It really depended on how hungover she was. We were not allowed to leave the house to go to school unless our beds were made, and our room cleaned. Dishes had to be done, lunches packed and any other chore my mom decided needed to be done. If we were late and missed the bus, we had to walk to school. I think she set me up to fail so I would stay home and do whatever she wanted me to do. I was good at organizing and cleaning. This was very useful to her. I could do all the housework and watch the children while she drank and used her drugs.

Learning to be an organizer was just another way of maintaining a bit of control. I always feel better when things are in their place. I love to put them there too.

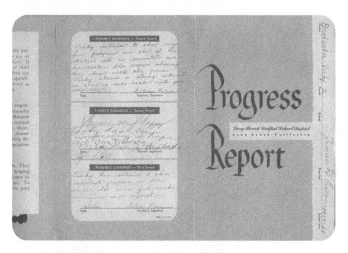

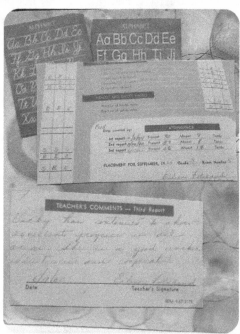

CHAPTER 20

My Hero

MY DAD WAS A JALOPY race car driver. He had the privilege of racing with many of the famous Jalopy drivers during the '50s and '60s. His best friend was Jack Kelly. He used to come to the house often, and I just adored him. He would always bring me little treats and greet me with a hug. Jack got married and broke my young heart when I was about five years old. Next thing I knew his wife got pregnant. She hated him racing. She instinctively knew this would be the demise of him and their relationship. He agreed to drive in one more race and then settle into being a new husband and father. My Dad was racing with him on his last run. All my family went to the track to watch his final race. Jack Kelly had a fatal car accident while rounding the corner for one last lap. It indeed was his last race. My Dad was a pallbearer, and I cried all through the funeral. Throughout my life, I thought about him often and always with a smile. Recently my sister sent me some pictures that she had found when she moved. I anxiously looked through them. There it was a picture of Jack. It immediately brought tears to my eyes! I had never seen this picture of him. I recognized him immediately. It brought me comfort from a deep place in my heart.

The movie "Gentlemen Start Your Engines" featured many of the famous Jalopy drivers in the 50's and 60's. My dad's racing name was Jack Brake. He had gotten a copy of the film and previewed it in our living room. I can still remember seeing all those fantastic, famous men sitting there watching the movie, smoking cigarettes and drinking beer. They were slapping each other on the back and reminiscing about how dangerous it was. They were all so proud to be featured in this movie. His racing friends were my favorites. Such an exciting time. The noise at the track was so loud, and here it was in our living room with all these racers. I knew it was so extraordinary. The trophy girls were something I never forgot. They would strut out on the track with their high heels on. Bathing suits fitting tightly and showing off all their assets.

Watching in awe as they were walking towards the winners with their sashes on and handing the winners their trophies. Sashes became an obsession with me. I made them out of whatever I had handy and adorned them whenever possible. One time I was selling cookies for my brownie troop and I got to go down on the track. The announcer came over the loudspeaker and introduced me. The trophy girl came over and told everyone to buy cookies from me. I sold the most cookies in my troop that year. I felt sash worthy. I made myself a sash and wore it to the meeting. I am confident I was the most obnoxious winner ever. I am surprised anyone even liked me. I always had lots of friends though. I was always generous and fun to be with. Where did all that confidence come from?

CHAPTER 21

My Baby Brother

WHEN MY BROTHER WAS BORN, he was not wanted. It messed him up mentally for his entire life. He was so sweet and so lost. He never stood a chance. He was my favorite sibling.

When he was about 3 months old, my Mom decided she wanted to get to the bar. We usually had to sit in the car and wait hours for her to come out. It became easier to just leave us at home. I was instructed to wash the car while she was gone. I had my best friend over at the time, Yvonne. She had eight brothers and no sisters. We hung out together a lot, because of her large family she was able to spend time away from her home. Since she had older brothers, she was much more worldly than I was. She thought it would be a good idea to take the car out for a little ride.

We were in 6th grade. I loaded up my new brother and wrapped him in blankets. She drove the car and off we went. We wanted to drive down nearby Shell Hill. It was the steepest hill in our town. We went down it a couple of times. We then headed back home. The neighborhood kids noticed we were driving and went in to tell their parents. One of them called the police. I washed the car as if nothing had happened. Suddenly the police knocked on my door. They wanted to talk to my Mom. I called her at the bar, and she came home. They said that they had a report about us driving the car. I acted surprised at the allegation. They went out and felt the hood of the car. It was warm. That was easily explained as I had to move the car to wash it. That really didn't go over with the Police. I had to confess. I got in so much trouble. My mom had to get back to the bar. She would say when I get back you are really going to get it. That was always a fun way to spend your day waiting for your beating. She would come in after 2:00 a.m., drunk and get me out of bed for the punishment.

I learned to trust my instincts after that event. If it feels wrong it probably is.

CHAPTER 22

Curiosity Or Obsession?

I SORT OF HAD A little history with vehicles. Another time while spending time at the bar my mom left me alone in the car. I decided to find out what would happen if I took off the emergency brake. The vehicle was parked on a hill. You guessed it, the car crashed into the car parked in front of me.

I was hoping she wouldn't notice. When she came out of the bar, to my surprise, she noticed.

Another time we had just got a new Mercury Montclair. It had white leather upholstery with an automatic cigarette lighter. Being curious I wondered what would happen if I pressed the hot lighter into the leather padding. I put a big burn in the seat. My butt burned too after my spanking. Lots of spankings were received over my messing with cars. I cannot believe that I took my little baby brother in that car with my eleven-year-old friend driving for the first time. Those neighborhood kids were such tattletales. God indeed was always watching over me.

My curiosity got the best of me again. One time I wanted to see what would happen if I tried to stop the mixer blades while the mixer was running. I turned it on and put my hand on the edges as they whirled around. My hand suddenly became one with the mixer. I unplugged the hand mixer. My hand would not come out no matter how hard I tried to get the blades off. My mom had to take me to the Dr.'s office for him to untangle me. I'm pretty sure that was the last time I was curious about that sort of thing. That was a painful experience. A spanking was received when I got home from the doctors office.

I switched to starting fires. Just small ones at first. I liked the smell of the fire. I would make a small one and then put it out. It quickly became more substantial as the days went by. I did it on the side of the house. It was the perfect spot. No one could see me, and there was a ton of stuff stored there. One day the fire got out of my control and charred the side of the house. I kept the hose with me to put the fire out. This was the first time I had to use it. Fear consumed me. That was the end of starting fires for me. I can't believe how stupid that was. I still wonder why I would do that.

About a year later my Mom decided it was time to clean up that side of the house. She found the charred part where I nearly burned the house down. She wanted to know what happened and who did it. If no one would confess, she would just spank us all until one of us would take responsibility. I admitted to it, but I really did not see any reason to discipline me. I had done that a year ago and I didn't start fires anymore. I mainly handled that situation a year ago. That was definitely old news. She did not see it that way. When my Dad got home, I got a severe spanking. Bent over, pants down and a leather belt, if you cried, you got more. I never even wanted to smoke a cigarette after that. To this day I never volunteer to use matches. I also don't like to start the fireplace or barbecue. That is called learning your lesson the hard way.

After all my experimenting with what would happen if I did this or that I let my mind wander elsewhere. I became obsessed with mixing up things to see the results.

It was my sister's birthday. I went shopping with my Mom to get her some birthday presents. Now I knew full well that she liked those plastic horses. She had them all over our room. I did not like them. To me they were nothing more than dust collectors. I picked out gifts for her that I would want. The perfume making kit was something I had coveted for months. I insisted that my sister had told me she wanted it so bad. I even volunteered to wrap the present for her. My mom was usually drunk and was happy that I would just take care of it. Opening her birthday presents could not come quick enough for me. I let her play with it for about an hour. I took it over and told her she was not doing it right. That was fine with her. She had very little interest in it. anyway. Becoming a perfume maker became my passion. Scents were all I thought about. Flowers were smashed up to get the oils from them. Kitchen cupboards became a plethora of possibilities. Especially the extracts and food coloring. They all became new items to sell at my fashion shows and beauty pageants. Yeah, I loved my sister's birthday gifts. She managed to amass a vast collection of those horses in spite of me trying to sabotage her.

When Barbie got a new sister, Midge, I convinced my sister she had to have it. After all, Midge was Barbie's little sister, and she was my little sister. Was there any question? I convinced her she needed it. She agreed, and she got Midge for one of her birthdays. She was bored with her new doll within minutes, she went back to the horses, and I had a new doll to play with.

This opened all kinds of new adventures for me. Midge needed her own bedroom in the cardboard playhouse. I went straight to work on accessorizing her and building her own bedroom. It was all about making her feel comfortable in her new bedroom. As far as I was concerned Midge needed a pet. My collection of pipe cleaners came to the rescue. A poodle was quickly made. Leashes, food, bowls, collar, and dog bed were quick to follow. Yes, Midge loved the new digs that I had made her inside the cardboard boxes. She was the same size as Barbie, clothes were readily available. She just needed to learn how to share. Barbie was generous with Midge, just as my sister should always be with me. I even had a field trip to the stables with my Barbie Family. They would not fit on the horses that my sister collected, so they could not ride them. Once again I was convinced the horses were stupid to me.

I was a manipulator to get what I wanted. Was that a good or bad thing? Maybe a little of both!

CHAPTER 23

Visions

WHEN I WAS YOUNG, I used to have visions of things. Mostly in my dreams. One time I was sitting in my swing in the backyard and I saw tons of angels, and they were all surrounding me. It was so comforting, and I felt so full of gratitude for my life. On another day I saw one of our birds, a bobwhite quail, die in my dream the night before. In the morning when I went out to feed him, he was dead. I was starting to get freaked out. I had a premonition that John F. Kennedy died also. Within two days of that vision, he was assassinated. Not knowing any better I thought I was causing these things to happen. It really scared me. I pushed those feelings way down deep inside of me. I knew things were going to happen when I had a vision. That's a lot of responsibility for a young child. They never talked about stuff like that in church. I did not want that kind of power. I had a lot of other things to worry about, like surviving.

I was a thinker. I could think about all kinds of possibilities. I have to say that is a good thing for me. I have learned to stay on the more positive side of thinking. Turning bad thoughts into good ones. Oh, the possibilities.

The Miami Herald

KENNEDY DEAD

Assassin Strikes in Dallas;
Lyndon Johnson President

DALLAS — (UPI) — President Kennedy was assassinated Friday. A single shot through the right temple took the life of the 46-year-old Chief Executive. He was shot as he rode in an open car in downtown Dallas, waving and smiling to a crowd of 250,000. Vice President Lyndon Johnson — the nation's new President — was in the same motorcade but a number of car lengths behind. He was not hurt.

Terribly shocked, Johnson, who has a record of heart illness, was whisked off under heavy guard to be sworn in as the 36th President of the United States.

Mrs. Jacqueline Kennedy was riding in the same car with her husband. She was not hurt. She cradled her husband's head in her arms as he was sped, dying to the hospital.

Kennedy was shot at approximately 12:30 P.M. CST (1:30 P.M. Miami time) and died at approximately 1 P.M. (2 P.M. Miami time). He was the fourth U.S. President to be killed in office.

Mrs. Kennedy Bends to Aid President (arrow), Slumped in Back Seat of Car After Assassination

An Editorial

'Did He Die? Oh, My God...'

Johnson Became Member Of Closely Working Team

CHAPTER 24

The Weekends

THE WEEKENDS WERE USUALLY A lot less stressful. We would go
out to eat on Friday or Saturday nights. My dad always picked
the restaurant. His favorites were Mexico City (best Mexican
food ever), The Coast Inn, a Steakhouse, and a Fish & Shrimp
restaurant, Prince of Wales. Living near the beach made it easy to
find delicious places to eat. These were some of my fondest times.
I got to have a Shirley Temple when I would go out with him. He
was always generous.

When my dad would come home on Friday nights, we would
usually have a dance party. He would turn the record player on,
and he would dance with my siblings and me. He often had a few
drinks by the time he had gotten home. He was in a very cheerful
and fun mood during our dance nights. I felt all the spotlights
were on me. I was the oldest and thought I could dance the best.

He was the reason I looked forward to these extraordinary
nights. It was always the highlight of my week. I could not imagine
anything more special.

I spent a lot of time on those days deciding which of the
albums we would listen to on our Hi-Fi stereo. Meticulously I
would pick out the perfect clothes to wear. I loved big full skirts
or dresses that would flare out while my Dad would be twirling
me around. I had washed and curled my hair so that it shined and
flowed all around when he would spin me. We both had big smiles

and laughed so jovially. I looked forward to every weekend that he lived in the house with us especially for dance night.

I still love dancing on the weekends! Even today I have a vintage record player. I put my albums from the '60s, '70s, and '80s on and dance the night away. I just love the crackle of the old needle hitting the vinyl. Happy moments were not very often. I treasured the dancing time and playing the albums.

Planning for these special times was the best of times for me.

CHAPTER 25

What Just Happened?

THE HOME WAS ABOUT TO turn upside down. My Dad was not living in the house. He had taken up residence with his new girlfriend. With her new freedom, my Mom was free to drink and drug all day and night. My ears were always listening for my Mom to beckon me to obey her commands. A note would be handed to me with two quarters. That meant it was time for me to go to the liquor store. I would walk as fast as I could so I could get back to my playing outdoors. I always walked with my head down while I would scurry to the store. I was on the prowl to find lost coins on the ground to get myself some candy. I would hand the note to one of the brothers that owned the liquor store. After reading the handwritten note, they would gather a pack of cigarettes and a large can of beer. If I had found any coins during my walk, I would peruse the candy counter and make my selections. They would ring up the transaction and then wrap it in a brown paper bag. I would pick it up from the liquor counter, and they would send me on my way. I would run home and give it to my Mom and head back outside.

My Mom loved talking on the phone while she would be getting drunk. I would keep track of how drunk she would be getting. When I felt she was out of it, and she was still on the phone, I would go and ask her if I could have a popsicle from the freezer. I would get one for myself and all my siblings. Interruptions were not well received. She would always say yes and dismiss me just so she could keep talking on the phone. One day I asked eight times for popsicles. Yes, I enjoyed eight popsicles in one day. Which meant my siblings all devoured eight popsicles too. Later in the day when she finally got off the phone, she stumbled over to the freezer to get some frozen food out for dinner. She noticed how many popsicles were missing. She asked me where they were. I explained that we ate them. I was quick to let her know she had given us permission to have the popsicles while she was on the phone. Without any hesitation, a quick slap in the face came to me. I was put on popsicle restriction. There were not to be any popsicles for me, not for a very long time. I was fine with that chosen punishment. In fact, I really did not care for popsicles. She made the popsicles with watered down kool-aid. They tasted like frozen colored water. I really liked the vanilla ice cream sundae cups. In the end, I came to realize that I had to always do things within reason. I tend to push things to the limit. I am pretty sure I just loved the recognition and the joy I received every time I came out with another popsicle. Even if permission were granted, it didn't excuse bad decisions.

I realized at that very moment I would have to govern myself. I needed to become my very own counsel. That lesson served me well. Be careful what you wish for.

CHAPTER 26

Always Entertained

THE DRIVE-IN THEATER WAS ONE of my Mom's favorite places to take all of us kids to. Before we would drive up to the ticket taker she would make us hide in the trunk of the car. That way she did not have to pay for all of us to get in to see the movies. After she parked she would come and let us all out. She could bring her liquor in and get drunk while watching two different movies. We would bring our own popcorn and lemonade. She was very frugal, she needed that money for herself.

She knew full well how afraid I was of rats and mice. The House On Haunted Hill was her choice of the film we would see one night. There was a scene in the movie where they strapped a cage with a rat in it to a man's face. The rat started eating the man's face. I was so freaked out that I started crying. I could not sleep that night from fear. She thought it was funny and told me I was too sensitive. It was at this point in my life that I discovered how to get through those kinds of days. I said to myself "It was just a moment and could not last forever." I could not control it, but I could control my reaction to it. I became the best feelings stuffer. It was amazing how much I could handle. I would not let her think she had gotten the best of me.

The Beatles were invading America. Boys from the neighborhood started letting their hair grow long. Beatle boots were in every male's closet. One of the girls who lived up the block had Beatlemania. She lived with her grandparents and was very spoiled. She had a Beatles record box filled with their 45's. She went to their concert and gave me every detail of the event. She screamed so long and hard she lost her voice. I didn't get it. Obviously she knew something I didn't. The Beatles were life changing, and that concert was iconic.

One day some of the neighborhood boys came to my house in their Beatle garb. My Mom invited them to come into the house. She gave them some of her little white pills. They could stay up all night with her and do whatever it was she did all night. They were instructed not to call their parents, and she invited them to spend the night. Their parents had no idea where they were. They each called the police to help find them. The police finally showed up at our house. It was the last place they knew that they had been earlier the day before. They were still awake and the boys were sent home. I had no idea they had spent the night.

My friend Yvonne, the car driver, spent the night often. My mom really liked her and shared her pills with her too. While at home she was telling her Mom that she had stayed up all night watching movies with my mom. Her Mom asked "didn't you get tired?" She said "No", that my Mom gave her little white pills and they would stay awake all night. I never took them myself, so I was unaware what was going on at night. My mom was providing sixth graders speed to stay awake and hang out with her all weekend long. Can you imagine? They were not allowed over to my house anymore. I was so embarrassed when I went back to school on Monday. I can't imagine why the authorities let these things happen. She should have been put in jail. I shuddered to think what was being said behind my back. I just tried to keep to myself.

There are so many more stories just like these. I do not know how I managed to get through those days. The good news is that days only come once in twenty-four hours.

Thank God for the church. The most beautiful family invited me to their church. They used to take me to church every Sunday. Phelps was their name and they had several tall boys. It was so helpful to me to get away from the madness of home. Praying was something I did not only at night on my knees, I prayed all day long. Please, Dear Lord, help me get through this day.

I never missed a Sunday. Bible Summer Camp was like Christmas to me. I went to it every summer. Every Sunday that I went to church I got an attendance certificate. For fifty-two certificates you could go to summer bible camp for free. I often wondered if they started that incentive just for me. I was usually the only one that earned all the certificates. There was no way I would ever miss a Sunday. Summer camp was the thing I looked forward to all year long.

My Mom complained that I would spend too much time in church. She tried to stop me from going all of the time. I begged her to let me keep going and my compromise was I would not attend all the extra activities that the church offered. I limited it to the events that I loved the most. I wanted to go to everything possible. I cried when I had to stay home. I had so much faith, I knew God kept me safe. I just wanted to give thanks. The refreshments were also a big plus for me. We did not get snacks like that at home and you could have as much as you wanted.

I loved the camaraderie too. No one wanted to hurt me. It was always such a safe loving place to me. I like to be around loving, kind people.

CHAPTER 27

Scary Car Ride

ONE DAY WE ALL LOADED into the car, and my Mom headed out on a new adventure. It was a bar called The Red Garter Saloon. She was in there for about four hours. Of course we had to wait in the car while she ran in for just a minute. We were restless and hungry. I went into the bar to try and get my Mom to come out and take us back home. I told her we were so hungry since we had not had anything to eat yet and it was well past noon. She reluctantly bought me one hot dog from the bar and sent me back out to the car. I split the hot dog into four pieces. I gave one piece to each of us to eat. There was this rule we had about sharing. One person would divide it, and the others got the first pick. That way we knew it was very equal. It was actually a great way to make sure you got your fair share. She was always skimpy with our food, so our portions were very important.

About an hour later she came out of the bar and got into the car. She could barely walk. She got into the car and started driving on the freeway going in the wrong direction. She had entered the freeway off ramp. So we were going against the oncoming traffic. I tried to tell her, and she was so drunk she would not listen to me. I begged her to get off the freeway. "I must go to the bathroom", I screamed at her. She told me to hold it. I told her I couldn't. I had to go now. She finally exited the freeway, and I pretended to go to the bathroom on the side of the road. I got back in the car and guided her to the correct on-ramp.

She started screaming at me. All of us children were just ungrateful bitches and bastards, and I was ruining her life. She then pulled into a Catholic Church. She went inside and told us to stay in the car. After about an hour I went inside to see what was going on. I saw her talking to the priest, and I overheard her say that she did not know which way to turn. I ran back to the car. When she got back into the car and started to drive home, I tried to tell her that I knew which way to turn to get back home. She told me to shut up. She knew the way home.

As I got older, I realized she was not looking for driving directions. She was looking for the path she should turn to for a better life. Obviously tortured and troubled she was miserable. When we arrived home, I knew that The Father, Son, and Holy Spirit was with me always but especially on the car ride home. It was the reason we were all still alive.

Yes, my faith was strong, and I believed in miracles. Every time we would get into the car I wanted to sit in the back and huddle in a ball on the floor. I did not want to see the crazy driving by the drunk woman. I just prayed to make it safely to each destination. My sister always wanted to sit in the front seat. I never could understand why. Cars did not come with seat belts. Her head went through the windshield more than once. Every car my mom ever had she crashed. It wasn't a matter of if she was going to have a car accident in this car, it was when? She even talked her friend into letting her borrow their vehicle once. Her car was in the repair shop and she wrecked their car too. She ran into a telephone pole. The police called the owners of the car and they came and took us home. I stopped counting how many cars she demolished after twenty five accidents. Yes, the safest spot while driving with my mom was on the floor in the back seat.

I found myself really frightened the day of that accident. I was still shaken up about it for a long time. I think when fear sets in that is your cue to step out.

CHAPTER 28

Puberty

MY DAD WOULD COME BY the house occasionally to have sex with my mom. That was the common thread that kept them together. They both shared a love of sex. Birth control pills were not available. My Mom was pregnant every year for about 12 years. She had 5 children, miscarriages, and several back-alley abortions. I remember going in the bathroom to use the toilet and seeing a fetus in the toilet. I had no idea what it was. I summoned my mom to see what it was. She scooped it up and off to the hospital we went.

The men seemed to make a beeline for her. I couldn't stand it. The worst part for me was when I started developing physically. I inherited her large breasts, thick hair, brown eyes, and long fingernails. These were all desirable assets to have in the early '60s. I always had a nice tan and blonde hair. I used iodine & baby oil to enhance my skin color because I was fair skinned. This was very attractive to the various men she brought home. They would frequently make sexual advances towards me. I would be at home babysitting while mom would be at the bar. The men would leave the bar and would come to our house and attempt to have sex with me.

Sometimes she would bring them home for sex so they would spend the night. After she passed out, they would try to crawl into bed with me. I always slept with one eye open. I was repulsed. I tried to tell my Mom, but she did not believe me. She said I was just jealous of her. This was a whole new situation I needed to be aware of.

I went to the thrift store with my friend and bought a bra. I thought this may help protect me. I hated wearing them. I was in 6th grade, and the boys would snap my bra strap. My sister would hide my bra from me. When boys came around, she would go get the bra and take it outside. While she would be roller skating, she would swing the bra above her head and yell out "Vicky wears a bra." I would just be so embarrassed. I was trying to hide my breasts and not announce to the world that I had them. She then hid my bra in the bathroom hamper. When boys would come over, she would take them to the bathroom and show them my bra. To me, this was just plain cruel. I could not find anything humorous about it. In her defense I am sure she did not know what I was going through. She was just looking for attention from these boys.

I was never comfortable having a curvaceous body. It brought attention to me. I am so much more comfortable being in the background. See me for what I do, not what I look like.

CHAPTER 29

The Day The Hatred Really Began

MY FRIEND, YVONNE'S FAMILY, HAD moved. We went to visit them one weekend. My Mom had already started drinking on the drive over to visit their new home. She was well on her way to being very drunk. We had not had anything to eat. When we arrived at their home she sent us on a walk to the nearest Taco Bell to get her some lunch. Whatever money was left over after we got her what she wanted, was ours. We got two tacos to split amongst the four of us children. We quickly walked back to deliver her food to her. We ate ours on the way back.

Yvonne's parents owned bloodhounds and kept them in cages in their backyard. The men in the family used the dogs when they would go hunting. My youngest brother wanted to see the dogs, and he climbed into their cage. They immediately attacked him viciously. He was screaming, and we went running out to see what was wrong. In that short amount of time that it took us to get outside, he was almost dead. The dog's were just doing what they were trained to do: attack and kill. By the time we got him out of the grips of the dogs mouths, his head and face were severely torn up. I pleaded with my mom to take him to the hospital. She said she would after she finished her lunch because she was hungry and still eating. I really thought he might die. I was hysterical with worry.

She finally finished her meal followed by another beer and then took him to the emergency room. They admitted him immediately and stitched him up. He stayed there for three days. He still has the scars on his face and head. Every time I look at him, it reminds me of how much I really hated her for that. She only cared about herself, alcohol, and drugs. Oh, and having her lunch.

I was getting older and began an intense hatred for her. I no longer looked at her as anything more than what she truly was. I did not like what I saw. I was beginning to compartmentalize my feelings.

CHAPTER 30

Moving On

IT WAS INEVITABLE THAT WE would have to leave our Signal Hill home. It was the longest time I had ever spent living in one place. My Mom didn't work and did not want to have a job. As is with most addicts they feel it is their job to get high. It consumes all of their time. I think when my parents got divorced, we went on welfare. My Dad had begun a new life with his new love and her family.

We packed up the house and got rid of most of our belongings. We then moved into a two-bedroom apartment in a poor neighborhood. You might give us the new title of poor white trash. While residing in our new apartment complex, my mom figured out a way to make some quick cash. She talked the owners of the complex, into letting her be the manager of the apartments. She would be responsible for collecting the rent and sending it to the owners. She initiated a new program for the tenants. If you paid your rent to her in cash, you would be rewarded with a discount. The money was collected by my Mom but never turned over to the management. She kept it for herself and it kept her well supplied in cigarettes, liquor and drugs. That would last for about sixty days until they would figure out, she was receiving the cash and keeping it for herself. We would get evicted and then she would move on to find her next rental management victims. There wasn't any way for the previous owners to warn others of what might be coming their way. There was not the benefit of the internet or any other social media. The people never pressed any charges against her because they felt sorry for us children. She played the victim card very well and it worked out nicely for her. We relocated about ten more times before she moved on to other schemes to get the money she needed for her drugs and drinking. I thought it was immoral and I was becoming increasingly embarrassed to be a part of this family.

I like to move around to meet new opportunities. I do not like running from past transgressions.

you'll never leave where you are until you decide where you'd rather be.

CHAPTER 31

Lucky To Be Alive

THE BARS MY MOM FREQUENTED were such a great place for her to meet men. She would take off and go on excursions with them for as long as she wanted to. As if she had no children. She would forget all her responsibilities and not return home for days at a time. No warnings, not any communication to say she would be gone for an extended period of time. She just would go out and not come home. There were rare times that she would leave the food stamps that she got from Social Services at home. She couldn't use them at the bars. I took advantage of this and used them for food. She did not do any grocery shopping for us before she would leave.

I was thankful for the little things like this. It gave me a resource for me to acquire food for us. I would not be able to attend school during these times. I couldn't leave my baby brother at home by himself. I had all of the responsibilities that a mother would have. Getting groceries, preparing meals, housekeeping, laundry and the welfare of four children. I was thirteen years old.

The only thing that bothered me was that I couldn't go to school. I missed school. My love of learning was growing stronger. I missed my daily schedule that school offered me. I never knew how long she would be gone and it weighed heavily on me. I wanted my siblings to be as comfortable as could be and a consistent schedule. When you live among chaos all you long for is structure. Some sort of control and boundaries.

One night my mom came home after four days of binging. She was high and very drunk. She woke me up in the middle of the night and pulled me out of bed and started beating me. There was always something that I had not done right. I don't remember if it was a dish in the sink or maybe all of the ironing was not done that set her off. She ripped my nightie off of me. Trying to escape her I started running and she then chased me out of the house almost entirely naked. I tripped and fell into the street. A car was driving by just at that same time. It was dark, and I was crying on the asphalt. She took her opportunity and tried to push my head under the tire of the passing car. The tires screeched and stopped the car before he hit me. Neighbors came outside of their homes to see what was going on and then called the police. My Mom went inside our apartment and passed out. I followed her in and composed myself.

It is exhausting I guess trying to kill your daughter. I went inside and got myself dressed. I cleaned my wounds, dried my tears and thought to myself welcome home Mom.

The police arrived and wanted to question my Mom to see what had happened. They tried shaking her and shined a flashlight in her face. They could not wake her. They told me I was probably safe for the night because they couldn't even wake her. I followed them to the living room and they left. Let's face it no one really cared about us.

I never hit my mom or tried to defend myself. Somehow though during the scuffle, I had scratched her. My Dad was coming over to visit the next morning. This explained to me why she had made it back home the night before. My Mom showed him the scratches that she had on her. She quickly told him I had done it to her and I needed a good punishment. He took me aside and asked me if I had scratched her. I said I did accidentally after she chased me outside and I was trying not to get my head squashed by the car. I basically was fighting for my life. I showed him my bruises and cuts and told him the police had been called to stop her. He went inside and said to her that he would not be punishing me because I did not deserve any punishment.

After he left, she was so angry at me for telling him the truth. Don't forget she always expected me to lie for her and all her dirty little deeds. She grabbed a big wrench and threw it at me. It hit me right in the eye. It caused a huge black eye on top of the other cuts and bruises from the night before. I went to school the next day looking pretty banged up. I told everyone I had been in another car accident. That was why I had been absent for so many days and why I was banged up. There are so many incidents like this, and they are hard to talk about. I find when I write about it my eyes always tear up. That's the thing about pain you can endure a tremendous amount. You can forgive but you somehow never forget it. I was greatful for the day to be over.

Responsibility for my siblings was a very heavy burden for me. I took my job seriously and always tried my best to protect them. I was loyal.

CHAPTER 32

The Big Reveal

MY NEW SINGLE DAD HAD started to make plans to take us kids on the weekends. He didn't want all of us at the same time, so he decided to take the boys first. The next week I assumed it would be the girls' turn. I started to get my things ready for his arrival when my sister informed me that I would not be invited to go with him. This made absolutely no sense to me, I did not understand that at all. Why wouldn't I be going? She went on to tell me that he was not my Dad, so why would he want to take me. Devastated by this lie she was telling me, I went to my Mom and told her what she had said to me. Why would she say this to me? She looked at me like I was stupid and said because it was true.

She was surprised that I ever thought he was my Dad. I wasn't going anywhere with him. She told me my Dad was the one I went to the hospital with when I was a young girl. The one and only time I had ever seen him, he took me to see my Grandmother before she died. I thought to myself, that was my Dad, that was my Grandmother? I guess I was glad to see them once.

I was so surprised. I was doing everything I could to figure this whole thing out. Before any of this news had settled into my brain, I was then told I was so sensitive and what was the big deal. Get over it, go help your sister get ready. Everything began to come into focus. It made sense why my stepdad treated my sister and brothers differently than me. Everyone acted like it was just another day.

He was an excellent stepdad to me. To his credit, I never really knew the truth. I never knew he wasn't my biological Dad. It was just hard not to be included. I realized I was a family of one. These people were all my stepfamily. No wonder I was always treated this way. I honestly did not belong. I was sad about that for a very long time. Nothing else was ever said about it. I thought my sister was cruel.

That is why I was always treated like the lame duck. No matter how hard I tried to be perfect I couldn't be. I didn't belong.

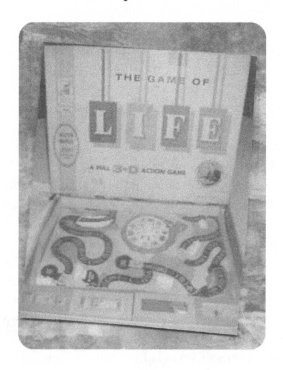

CHAPTER 33

Take Good Care Of Yourself

WHILE I WAS IN JUNIOR High, they gave us a mandatory Tuberculosis test. When the results came in, my test was positive. The health department came out to my home and picked me up to get chest x-rays. My results were positive. I most certainly had Tuberculosis. The health department gave my mom some protocol for me to keep me healthy. My Mom never took me to any of the appointments. I had to find my own way there. They put me on some medication, I took the pills eight times a day. I had to get chest x-rays every three months to watch my lungs. The x-ray technician was always the same man, and he gave me the creeps. He always needed me to get naked for the x-ray and wanted to touch my breasts. There was not a single reason why he would need to contact my breasts. I was there for chest x-rays, not a mammogram. I felt ashamed and very much alone. I remember leaving the clinic and had to walk home crying all of the way there. I went to the appointments by myself, no one really cared if I went or not. The technician creeped me out and I was never monitored. So, I stopped going. I would go and pick up my medicine, but I never got another X-ray from that creep.

Medical care was so easy going in the '60s. When I went to the dentist, I would get a certificate after my check-up for a free ice cream cone. He could pass out ice cream coupons, but he was a terrible dentist. There was always a treasure chest in the doctor's office. You got to pick out whichever little toy you wanted. The doctor would come in smoking a cigarette while he examined you. The dentist that I was taken to was a fellow alcoholic friend of my Mom. I had to have my entire mouth redone when I became an adult. He did more harm than good. At twenty-one years old my dentist told me he had seen ice cream cones constructed better than my fillings. I found the ice cream cone correlation ironic considering the ice cream cone coupons I was given after my visit to the dentist. As a child, I was never taught to brush my teeth at home. I thought it was just something I did when I visited my Granny. I did not start brushing my teeth regularly until I was sixteen years old. I did not get my teeth cleaned until I was twenty-one years old. Once I started, I could not believe that there were never any toothbrushes in our house. I realized that my Mom had dentures. She didn't need to brush. Why should we?

She was just a child in an adult body. She caused chaos wherever she roamed. I hate chaos.

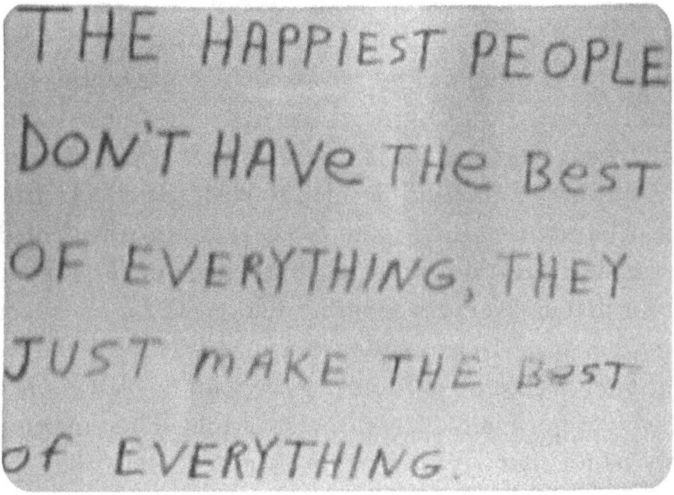

THE HAPPIEST PEOPLE
DON'T HAVE THE BEST
OF EVERYTHING, THEY
JUST MAKE THE BEST
OF EVERYTHING.

CHAPTER 34

Thou Shall Not Steal

On one of our "here's where we live this month adventures," my mom really went crazy. Our neighbor was a single mom. She was a widow, so she lived on a monthly check from Social Security. My mom was aware of this and decided to steal her checks from her mailbox. She tried cashing them for herself but was denied. She couldn't collect the money, so she burned them. This poor lady looked for that check every month. I felt so sad for her that I told her son what my Mom was doing. I mean this was their entire income. They would go without and depend on that money. She got a lock for her mailbox, and that was that. They never shared with my Mom that I was the one that told them that she was stealing their checks. I started getting my own voice. I began to know right from wrong on my own terms. I began to speak up!

One of her favorite nighttime activities was to go around and take things from other people's yards, garages, and outside laundry rooms. One morning we woke up to her car having smoke and flames all through it. It was on fire. The fire department came to put the fire out. The police showed up too. Then this man pulled up in his car behind the police. He demanded the police open our garage door. The man from the car began telling a story to the police. He accused my Mom of stealing his child's mechanical toy vehicle. He knew it was in her garage. Of course, he was right. The police made her open the garage door, and there it was. He took the toy car and loaded it into his vehicle. Under his breath, I heard him say that he got his car back and she lost hers. He was right. We were without a car for a long time. We finally got another car, and we moved again.

After that incident, I think the courts made my Mom go to a therapist. Maybe she decided on her own, but I remember her being required to go to the appointments. The counseling included her receiving shock treatments. She didn't much care for it, and indeed she did not want to change. She quit showing up for her appointments. I never noticed anything changing in her behavior.

The new neighborhood we moved into was very friendly. My Mom made a lot of new friends. This made it easier for her to take off and be gone for many more excursions away and for longer periods of time. She had plenty of men that she was dating. She was in her early thirties by now.

I began to feel tired of all of this responsibility and wanted some help. I wanted to start living my life not everyone else's.

CHAPTER 35

High School Love

I STARTED ATTENDING POLYTECHNIC HIGH School. I was about to meet a brand-new group of people. I never minded about changing schools and neighborhoods. I always felt like it gave me a clean slate. I kept my feelings and emotions to myself. I was very guarded and did not expose myself. No one would know my past and the embarrassment of living in my family. The whole family situation was getting harder and harder to hide. The same way that I tried to hide my big breasts, I tried to hide my current life. When you meet new people, they ask questions about your past. I frequently would change the subject. My student ID card picture shows just how bewildered I was.

I was fortunate to go to a high school that was very integrated. There was every ethnicity you could imagine. Interracial dating was common. The economic scale of the students was from very low to extremely high. There were a lot of very talented athletes that graduated into the professional field. It was such a great place for me because you could find your own niche quickly.

I started to be attracted to boys. I was still very guarded and put forth a lot of effort to protect my secrets of life at home. I always dressed very conservatively. I did not want to draw attention to my figure. To me having big boobs was a curse. I finally dated one extraordinary boy. He wanted to come over to my house and visit me. I did not want him to see where I lived or what was going on inside my house. I was embarrassed and thought people would judge me. I knew they would think that I would be just like my mother. If their parents would find out my background, they would never be able to see me again. I would wait until my Mom would go on her daily trip to the bar and then invite them in. It was a lot of work manipulating this out of control chaos into some sort of normalcy. I was always afraid she would unexpectedly show up. I gave up trying to date this boy. I broke up with him. I gave up so quickly on trying to make myself happy. It was easier to hide the truth than to experience the joy life has to offer.

I started dating someone that I could not resist. Ronny was tall, handsome, quiet and kind. I found him to be irresistible. He did not seem to be judgemental and I always felt safe around him. After all, he was the cutest boy in the whole school. We had an instant attraction.

The first date that we went on was a double date. The four of us went to the drive-in movies. We had brought a bottle of champagne with us. I had never indulged in alcohol before. I toasted to our first date with the champagne. I became inebriated very quickly, and I do not remember anything after that. Ronny dropped me off at my home after our first date. I can't even tell you what movie was playing. I saw him at school the following Monday. He reluctantly showed me his neck. I could see that I had given him hickeys all over his entire neck. I didn't even remember kissing him, let alone smothering him with all those hickeys.

Ronny was wearing a turtleneck sweater to hide them. It was a warm day and he was quite uncomfortable. He did his best to hide them. His mom was so mad at him for coming home with all that mess on his neck. Can you imagine what she was thinking about me? I was so embarrassed and thought I would never see him again. I was so grateful that he did not give up on me. We went steady for three years. I have never had another glass of champagne since that first date.

One of the highlights of my life that I had lived thus far was when Ronny asked me to be his date for the prom. The theme was beyond the looking glass. I did not have anything to wear to such a fancy affair. I started looking at thrift stores for a suitable gown to wear.

As if the skies parted and God sent from heaven two angels for me. Two friends that I had met at school, Pam and Laurie, showed up at my house with everything I needed for that dream date. Prom dresses to choose from, shoes and jewelry. It was just like having two fairy godmothers and I was Cinderella. They wanted me to have anything I would use. It was so precious, loving and generous. I have never forgotten their extreme kindness and thoughtfulness. They lived in very nice neighborhoods, had their own cars and were both beautiful girls. They were not the kind of people I was used to having around me. When they pulled up, I was overwhelmed. I hated for them to see where I lived. I was so grateful but mostly embarrassed. I have recently been in contact with one of those fairy godmothers. I told her how I could never forget how much their kindness meant to me. I also let her know that I was so embarrassed about where I lived. She said to me that they liked me for who I was, not for where I lived. They appreciated my willingness to be so open with them. They were insecure about who they were just as I was but for different reasons. I suddenly realized that it is a typical teenage feeling. It doesn't matter who you are. They felt they could be themselves around me. I cried. What a waste of time being embarrassed for much of my life.

My heart is still so full of love from that one day in my life. Life was looking up.

CHAPTER 36

Love

I WAS SO GRATEFUL TO have a beautiful dress to wear. My boyfriend's mother was a hairdresser, and she did my hair for me. I felt like a real princess. I felt my lips were sparkling and my cheeks looked rosier. My hair looked so pretty, and I was so proud that his Mom had made me look so beautiful. I had my handsome prince, and I was going to the prom. He was in a tuxedo and looked like a movie star. A girl like me never dreamed of becoming so beautiful, being surrounded by so much love. I felt that I had on the prettiest dress of everyone at the prom, given to me by the most amazing girls. My beautiful hair was styled, and hair sprayed to stay put! I was just sure I had diamonds sparkling in my eyes. Ronny was the most handsome I had ever seen him. He arrived with a fragrant corsage for me. The aroma from the flowers on my wristlet corsage was all the perfume I needed. Wow, I could not have dreamed of a better night. It didn't matter what I would face when I went back home, this was my night. This is the fairytale all girls dream about. I still have my dried corsage and prom tickets. Our picture together at the prom is still the cutest couple in the world. The most precious thing I have though is the memories.

My life started to turn around after that. I went out on another date with Ronny. After our date together that night he took me home. I bent over and kissed him. I thanked him for a wonderful time, and I began to get out of the car. He stopped me and told me to go inside and gather all my belongings. When I was finished, he told me to come back to the car. He was taking me home with him to live at his house. He said it with such authority that of course, I did it. When we got to his house, he told his mom I would be living with them for a while. She gave up her bedroom and slept on the couch. I could not believe what she had done for me. I could not believe what I had done. I could not believe what he had done for me. For some reason, I trusted him though. After all, I was fifteen years old, and he was sixteen. Ronny's dad had left his mom when he was young. He had taken on the role of being the man of the house. This all seemed so natural.

Somehow even though he was young, he seemed so mature. I loved being there with his Mom and him. I got breakfast in the morning, a ride to school and my own room. Life was good. It was the first time in my life I felt safe and secure. I didn't ever want anyone to feel sorry for me. I just thought that I had gotten all the bad things out of my life early and the rest was up to me. It meant that I could choose how to live the rest of my life just the way I wanted to. And I decided to live a life full of happiness and adventure. I felt like I had already gone through all the bad things that would be coming to me in this lifetime and I was going to be happy every single day from there on out. I felt relief, but I knew it could be taken away from me at any time. Since my mom was alive, I never felt entirely at ease.

I had a ton of guilt for leaving my siblings. I felt I had abandoned them. I really felt responsible for their wellbeing. I took it seriously, and I cared for them like a mother with her children. I hoped that with me not being there to do everything, my Mom would stay home and take care of her responsibilities. Knowing the person, she was, that was more of a fantasy of mine than any kind of reality. She decided my sister could take over after I was gone. She was almost ten years old. My brothers were six years and four years old. What she didn't realize was that my sister was not me. She was used to being taken care of by me. She had never been beaten by anyone in the family. She was daddy's little girl. She had a dad that she could reach out to for love and support. I didn't have any family to be there for me to turn to. I told myself everything would be just fine.

For the first time in my life, I felt loved. My boyfriend made me feel special. I was a virgin, and so was he. It was a natural progression to experience love making together. We were always alone at his Mom's house, and we took advantage of it. We were so close. I was loved, I felt safe, I had someone who cared about me. I wanted it to be forever. This man was my salvation. I never wanted him to leave me. In my mind, this was forever. I would go to the grave loving this man and all he had done for me.

The phone calls from my siblings started coming to me. They wanted me to move back into the house. Guns were being shot in the home by my Mom's new boyfriend. They needed me to calm everything back down. My boyfriend, Ronny received calls from my siblings. Most of them he never told me about. He protected me from all the drama I had previously lived with. By this time my mom was in her early thirties. She had met a new boyfriend at the bar. They planned to marry. He was 29 years old, and he was a virgin. I felt sorry for him. He inherited her children and all the chaos that went along with it. Her new husband wanted a child of his own. My Mom got pregnant and wanted me to move back home. Since she was pregnant and married, she was staying home more often. She was beating on the other children now. She continued drinking, drugging and smoking while she was pregnant. The police were being called out to the home for child abuse more frequently. Finally, social services stepped in. They would come out to the house to check and see if the children were being taken care of. Because she was on welfare, they wanted to know where I was. This was the perfect excuse to make me come back home. She would come to my school and insist that she wanted me to leave school and go home with her. The administration officials knew of my circumstances because I worked in the office during one of my classes. The office would send a call tag for me with a note on it that would say: "You have permission to leave the school grounds because your mother is here." The call tag would then be returned to the office. The teacher would comment that I was not in class and she was told I was not there. She got so angry and frustrated. My Mom was not used to me not obeying her. The police would be called nightly by my Mom telling them to come and get me and return me home. They knew her because of all the calls to our home, so they never came and got me.

My life was feeling pretty darn good. The school was protecting me and making sure my Mom could not get to me. The police were protecting me by not arresting me and making me go back home. My boyfriend, Ronny defended me like a lion with his cub. Ronny's mom protected me and cared for me. Ronny kept me safe, he loved me. The sex and intimacy was incredible.

All my needs were being met. This was the beginning of my joyful days and the end of the miserable ones. Thank you, God.

CHAPTER 37

Sad

SEVERAL CONCERNED NEIGHBORS CALLED CHILD Protection Services on my mom. The children were finally removed from the home. I don't know where their Dad was because I wasn't there. They finally took them away from my Mom. That meant all her income was also removed. She called and begged me to help her get the children back. Because I hated to see the children hurt I did help her. It broke my heart seeing them in protective custody. I felt responsible and terribly sad. She got them back quickly. Shortly after they returned the children to her care, she moved out of Long Beach. My pregnant Mom, her new husband, and all the children moved to Orange County. As soon as she got moved into their new house, she called the Orange County police and filed a report with them that I was a runaway. She wanted them to pick me up and arrest me. She gave them the address of where I was staying. That evening the police showed up at Ronny's house. They had come to arrest me and take me to jail. Ronny's Mother was so compassionate and explained to them what was going on. They wanted to put handcuffs on me and walk me out to the police car. His Mother asked them to please not do that! She assured them I would not cause them any problems. They took me to the Long Beach jail first to wait for them to take me to Orange County. Long Beach was very familiar with my Mom. She would get drunk and report me as a runaway daily. The police there were so kind to me they were on my side. They told me they had tried to prevent the other county from coming to get me. Because they didn't know her they came to arrest me. I was then transported to Orange County jail. My Mom reported to the police that I was incorrigible and tough to handle. I was placed in solitary confinement at the facility because of the report my Mom had given to the police. They were prepared to deal with a very unruly runaway teenager. I remember feeling sad, lonely and cold.

While in confinement, I asked for a pen and paper to do some writing to my boyfriend. I was given a broken pencil and one sheet of paper. I wrote down all of the feelings that I could fit on that one piece of paper, front and back. I knew Ronny would come and rescue me. That is what your heroes do for you. After being in custody for one day, my Mom showed up and asked if I was ready to go home and behave? I wanted out of jail, so I said yes. As soon as we got home, she and her new husband went straight to the bar. Once again, her babysitter and housekeeper was back. She was free to get back to her drinking and all was well with her. I called my boyfriend to let him know that I had been sprung. He was at work and said he would pick me up as soon as his shift was over. I gave him the address and prepared for my departure. As soon as I hung up from talking to Ronny, my Mom gave me a courtesy call from the bar. She told me I better be getting ready, as soon as she got home, I was going to get the beating of my life. I had better have the house cleaned and dinner ready too. I hung up the phone and decided not to wait for my boyfriend to pick me up. He was working late, and I didn't know when my Mom might show up. I did what she said I should do "Get Ready". I started walking from Orange County back to Long Beach. It was a twenty-five-mile hike. I was so determined to get back to the safety zone that I was going to do it. I walked back to my boyfriend's house. I stayed there, and the police never came back looking for me again.

I felt safe for a while.

CHAPTER 38

Truth

My boyfriend, Ronny decided I should find my biological Father. That was an exciting turn of events. I asked some of my mom's friends if they knew anything about him. They were more than eager to share with me what they knew. My father was managing a nightclub in Sunset Beach. I don't know how Ronny located him, but he did. He gave my boyfriend a job cooking at the nightclub. He wasn't really looking for a job but he thought it was a good way to get close to him. I didn't know what to expect. I had only met him once. I had no idea what he even looked like. Let's just say he was not a Father Of The Year candidate.

My boyfriend got to know him before I did. My Father was fun, witty, and had a great sense of humor. Everyone seemed to like him and he had a lot of friends. He was wildly entertaining, and he loved dancing. I learned about my uncle Fred and aunt Laverne from my Father's stories. He had so many stories to tell. He was very charismatic. His brother and sister had been invited to dance in front of the King and Queen of England. My father had danced in movies, won numerous competitions, and is a Hall Of Fame Dancer. He was a fantastic dancer. I wished I had been able to learn to dance, or even had a dance with him. I had always wanted to learn how to dance. When I was young, I begged my mom to let me go to dancing classes. After much coercing she took my sister and me to a dance studio. We went for a trial class. The teacher said I had talent, but my sister did not. The teacher felt it would be a waste of money for my sister to take lessons. She would like to work with me though. I was so excited. My mom drove us home, and we never went back. When I asked about when I would be starting classes, she told me that if both my sister and I didn't go neither of us would go. I cried so hard that night. I practiced the steps I learned in that class every chance I could. I still know those steps to this day. I wanted to learn but the timing wasn't right for me. I used to watch the afternoon dance shows that were on TV. I learned from them the best I could. I did finally go to some classes as I got older.

Ronny's mother came to the conclusion that we had been having sex. She decided it was time for me to move because she did not want me to get pregnant. We were too young to be starting a family. It did not stop us from being intimate, but it sure did slow us down. She had found a charming family for me to go and live with. I did not want to leave, and Ronny did not want me to go either. Lots of tears were shed, but his mom had made her final decision. Ronny and I had nothing but respect for her. She had been very generous to help me as much as she did. I still have the utmost respect and love for her. She sacrificed for me because of her love of her son. She did whatever she could to make him happy. I feel so blessed to have spent the time with her.

I moved in with the new family that she had arranged for me. They really were a perfect family. We were so far apart in the personality department. It was tough for me to relate and fit in. He was a doctor, and she was a stay at home mom. They had a lovely house with a pool. They let me stay in their daughter's room. She had just gone away to college. They had rules and a different way of living than I had ever experienced. They had hamburgers and chocolate shakes every Friday night. They took me to Vacation Village in San Diego for a family vacation. I had never been on a family vacation. I had no idea about this sort of thing. I missed my boyfriend and felt so out of sync with these kind folks. They could not have been more loving and helpful to me. I just didn't know how to fit in. I had never experienced this family dynamic before, and it was hard for me to find my place. I tried my best, but I left their family after about 6 months. I just couldn't adapt to this environment. It was such a strange thing to experience. My needs were all being met by this family that did not even know me. I felt unworthy of their love and generosity. I often think about them and wish I could tell them how grateful I was, and I really felt sorry for hurting them when I moved out. I just felt like a square peg trying to fit into a round hole. When you have been treated a certain kind of way all of your life it is what you come to expect. You are broken and you are searching for other broken people to make you feel whole.

Love is unconditional but sometimes it is elusive. I felt very unworthy. I never expected this from complete strangers. I did not know how to reciprocate.

CHAPTER 39

Home Schooled

RONNY USED TO WALK ME to each of my classes and made sure I was safe inside before he would run off to his classes. He would be at the door waiting for me when class was over too. One of my teachers would always let me know when my "bodyguard" was there to pick me up. It had become increasingly difficult to go to high school because my Mom's visits were becoming more frequent. She didn't call the police anymore she would just come to my school and tell them she needed to take me home. They always told her the same thing, "she is not here". But each time she came I would have to leave the school grounds to make it true. I was missing a lot of classes. Once again, she was pregnant and she needed my help. My teachers were so supportive of me and would bring my assignments to me. They all knew the situation at my home. They had seen the bruises and black eyes. They had encountered her at meetings also. I was doing all my schoolwork at home and turning it into the office every week. I didn't realize how many people thought I was worth something. This was true dedication on their part. These were teachers who cared about teaching. They cared about helping me. They thought I was worth it.

I missed all the social interaction and all the friends I had made at school.

My Order to the Universe

Name VICKY

Date

With Much Gratitude I Allow The Universe To Bring M

1	love on my terms
2	abundance
3	worthiness
4	Patience
5	Happiness

Received by The Abundant Universe

CHAPTER 40

Set Free

I MOVED IN WITH MY friend Robin's family that I went to High School with. Robin's mom was sympathetic to my situation. Not only did she let me live with them, but she also shared with me that I could become emancipated from my family. With my permission, she filed all the paperwork for me. She also paid for all of the legal expenses. A court date was set. I went to court on the day that had been scheduled to decide if I would be set free. I was so nervous and dreaded the thought of seeing my Mom. Luckily for me, she did not show up to court. We didn't get to hear her reasons why I should continue to live with her. The judge said because she was not present for the proceedings that I was granted emancipation. He said if she couldn't bother even showing up she defaulted. I could not believe that she gave in so quickly. She must have been hung over and couldn't get out of bed I thought. The judge gave me the responsibility to govern myself. She could no longer tell me what to do. She could not control me or where I would live.

No more beatings or verbal abuse. No more worries about being arrested for being a runaway. I was able to go back to High School, attend classes and graduate. I have to say that my teachers in High School were so supportive. They helped me through such a hard time. They saw something in me that I didn't even see in myself. Without the teachers bringing my schoolwork to the house and giving me tests, it would not be possible for me to graduate with my class. I was given a cap and gown as a gift from the school. I was able to accept my diploma, and walk across the stage with my friends.

While living with Robin's family, I received my daily telephone call from Ronny. It would be at the sametime every day to make sure I had gotten home safely from school. He was older than me and had a job while I was finishing High School. One day he didn't call me. I just knew at that moment something was different. The next day he called right on time. I was so relieved to hear his voice. He wanted to let me know that we would not be seeing each other anymore. Ronny had decided to break up with me. When we stopped living together, he did not feel the same way about me. He thought I could take care of myself and that he was not needed. That was not how I felt. I believed we were going to be together until the day I died. It was the day before my birthday and the weekend before my prom. It was two weeks before my graduation. He offered to still escort me to all of these events. I politely said it would not be necessary. I hung up the phone and started crying. How could this happen to me when my life was finally becoming my own? I had to carry on as I had done so many other times. This time it was much harder for me because I loved him so much. I had a lot of things to prepare for as my high school days were ending. It was with a very heavy heart that I continued moving on. Ronny had left me but I was not going to leave myself. I had things to do now on my own. I knew this scenario all too well.

It was when I began to realize what was to be expected of me. I would need to take care of myself. I truly had been set free.

C H A P T E R   4 1

Bittersweet

As I proudly walked across the stage and graduated, I did not have one person to watch me in the audience. No cards or gifts were waiting for me. Family & loved ones were not there to congratulate me. Most importantly I did not have Ronny by my side. I was planning on spending the rest of my life with him, and he wasn't there. I was devastated. I cried every night for a month. I burned all the pictures of us together. My knight in shining armor had tarnished. I was no longer a princess.

I finally got the nerve to call his house after weeks of not being able to find any relief from this heartache. I was looking for answers as to why this had happened. I was really hoping for a reconciliation. The phone was answered by his mom. She quickly said he was not there. I remember her telling me he was getting married and that I should not call him ever again. It was like a nightmare that I wanted to wake up from. We had never even had a fight ever. What had I done wrong? How could he be getting married when we had only been broken up a few weeks?

One of Ronny's friends finally explained it all to me. He told me that Ronny's future wife was pregnant. He was going to do the right thing and marry her. That explained everything to me. He had been cheating on me and got her pregnant. Knowing the type of man he was, I was not surprised that he took responsibility for his actions. Disappointed and devastated I picked myself up and started to live my life without him. I missed everything about him. I never got over him. He had made such an impact on my life. He loved and protected me at a time that I was desperate for both of those things.

My first love was now a memory. I did not call him again, and we never talked about it.

CHAPTER 42

On My Own

ONE THING I HAVE LEARNED from all my life experiences so far is that you cannot want something for someone else more than they want it for themselves. I couldn't make my Mom stop drinking, I couldn't make my Father want me, and I couldn't make my boyfriend stay with me. People must want it for themselves. You cannot change anyone but yourself. I have also learned that it is up to me how I choose to react to others. When people treat you in a judgmental way, it indeed is their problem. I cannot let it be my problem. I am the only one who can choose how my life is going to turn out. I have decided to be happy every day. I would not let anyone steal my joy. I had already lived unhappy, and I did not enjoy that. Feeling miserable does not hurt anyone but me. It is my choice to live happily and not take on other people's feelings. My day is mine and I can have a great day or I can have a bad day. It is all up to me.

When I was in a bookstore, I discovered Edgar Cayce. I found a book he had written and read it cover to cover. If you haven't heard of him, here's a little bit about his background. He was a sleeping prophet. He made many predictions when he would go into a sleeping trance. His assistant would take notes on what he was saying in his sleep and read them to him when he awoke. Many of the predictions he made have come true. He was very active in the 1920s. He opened my eyes to the psychic world. I began to be more comfortable with my own visions. I was more mature and realized that I was not causing these things to happen. I merely was seeing the things that could happen. I was not suppressing these thoughts any longer I was embracing them.

I started dating someone new. My new boyfriend, Neil was so sweet and kind. His family was very welcoming too. A perfect gentleman. It was time to move out of Robin's house. I was 18 years old, and it was time to grow up. I always say that it was the first day of my new life. I got several jobs to support myself.

I was working at a donut shop, a pharmacy, and a Chinese food restaurant. I depended on friends and public transportation to get to work. There was very little time to sleep. I started saving for a car. I found a small house for 87.50 a month. It was above a couple of garages and behind the home of my friends Kevin and Carol. No one ever prepared me for all of this responsibility. I didn't know how to get a good job, pay bills, find a place to live or get a car. I felt this would have been a good class for all seniors to take: How to live on your own. I know I would have taken it.

I did not know what to expect and I did not have any parents to get advice from. I had to figure it out. I learned not to depend on anyone but myself.

EVERYO
NE HAS
A STORY

CHAPTER 43

Disgusting

ONE MORNING WHILE WORKING AT the donut shop one of my regular customers asked if I had gotten a car yet. I said no, I was still saving for it. He said he would like to buy me a car. He also wanted to help me pay my rent. There are lots of girls who do things like this, he said. I would be like your Sugar Daddy. What is that I wondered? He began to explain it to me. He would do things for me, and in exchange, I would do things for him. I thought he was talking about maybe a loan that I would repay.

No, he told me I would not ever have to pay him back. "So, what kind of things would I do for you to pay you back?" I asked. He explained that I could provide him with sexual pleasures. The thought of even touching him made me want to throw up. I immediately felt so sick to my stomach. He told me to think about it, and we could go car shopping the next day. I excused myself and went into the bathroom and threw up. I did not care if my shift was over or not. I walked out of that shop and never returned. I felt so gross. I kept thinking to myself, what am I doing to encourage men to be attracted to me. I struggled with it and did not like it at all. I never dressed provocatively. I had big boobs, so I always covered them up. I did not wear makeup. I wore thrift store clothes. To be honest, I did not know what these men saw in me. It was such a mystery to me. I really did not have anyone to talk to about it. Ronny had always protected me from this sort of thing. I couldn't call him to rescue me. I realize now that without having parents to guide me, I had a lot of unanswered questions. What is going on? What am I doing to provoke this? This is very disturbing. I became embarrassed. Once again I felt it was all my fault.

If you feel something is not right it usually isn't. But it was not my fault.

> # If I ever
>
> tell you about my
> past, it's never because
> I want you to feel
> sorry for me,
>
> but so you
> can understand why
> I am who I am.

CHAPTER 44

The Car Situation

NEIL WAS PLANNING A BACKPACKING trip with another friend of ours, Tom. Tom went to high school with us. He also worked as a manager at the ice cream store three doors down from the Chinese restaurant that I worked at. We would exchange Chinese food for banana splits. I was never even thinking that was really stealing from the owners. When I look back on it now, I feel bad because it was wrong. A parent's guidance could have come in handy. I had received my moral foundation from the church, but sometimes things are not that simple. There was not a book with right and wrong things to do. I mostly trusted my instincts. I was learning about life in the big world. I was trying to make the right choices. I realized that different choices could have brought on wrong decisions too. I learned to live with the choices I had made and the only reason I should look in the rear view mirror was to see how far I had come.

Tom had the cutest 1954 V.W. bug. He knew I did not have a car. He offered to loan me his car while Neil and him were on their backpacking trip. I could not believe my luck. I could drive to all my jobs! That meant more time for me to sleep. They were gone for about a month. I got used to that little car, and I really loved it. They had returned from their backpacking trip. I called Tom to deliver his car back to him. I washed and cleaned it. I filled it up with gas and prepared to be a walking girl again. He said he would be home all day getting ready for a party that he was having at his house that night. I asked if he could use my help to get everything ready. He said he would love my company and welcome the help. I appreciated the car loan so much. I did not do much to help with the party. I just kept him company. I realized that I had started to have feelings for him. I am not sure if I liked his kindness or the generous loan of the car.

Neil met me at the party. He was going to give me a ride home. I had not seen him since he returned from his trip. I told him I did not want to be in an exclusive relationship any longer. I wanted to date others. He did not take it well. He immediately left the party without me. Guess who needed a ride home? Steve, a friend of ours, was dating Robin. She was the girl I had been living with while I was in high school. He offered to give me a ride after he dropped her off. Tom wanted to ride along with us. Tom & I got into the back of our friend Steve's van. We arrived at Robin's house. Steve got out and walked her to the door. Tom and I jumped out of the van to get into the front. While outside, before getting into the front seat we shared our first kiss. Since it was our first kiss, it was kind of a long one. Steve quickly jumped in the van and took off. He did not even notice that we were not in the van with him. He came back to get us, and we were still kissing. We jumped in and off we went to take me home.

There is nothing like a new friend to help you forget an old one.

CHAPTER 45

I Like A Quiet Man

TOM ASKED IF HE COULD spend the night and I said yes. He spent the night. We did not have sex. From that day on he never left my house. We never dated, we just started living together. He was twenty years old, and I was eighteen years old. I lived by myself for about four days.

Friends had told me that he had an STD and I should not be intimate with him. I assured everyone that I was not having sex with him. We used to call it balling. It sounds so funny. Before we ever had sex, he asked me what birth control I was using. I said I had never used anything other than the rhythm method. On one of our first dates, he took me to the free clinic for birth control. We both got tested for any sexually transmitted diseases. It turned out that the girl he had been dating didn't like him ditching her for me. She lied to him and told him she had a venereal disease. It would be in his best interest not to have a relationship with me. She really did not have an STD, and neither did he. I knew I didn't because I had been a virgin when I first was intimate with Ronny and so was he. He had been my only sex partner. Our tests both came back negative, and I walked out with birth control pills. That said to me that we were headed for the next step. Tom kept his emotions to himself. He quickly told me that he did not want me to speak of my past. He made it clear that he wanted me to keep whatever was on my mind to myself. He always did the same. I was quite used to this coming from the family that I did.

Tom was very quiet. I like that in a man. He was shy and did not seem to have a lot of confidence. A bit awkward, not a lady's man. He didn't speak much, but when he did, it appeared to be important. He had a dry sense of humor, often misunderstood. He loved the outdoors, and his long legs made him a natural walker. His passions were for backpacking, camping and just being in nature. I had never done any of those things. I really did not know very much about the world in general. Most of my life so far has been about surviving. Everyday average life moments were not familiar to me. I was used to reacting to situations, not creating them. I was interested in the new adventures he spoke of. He lived in the moment and was not motivated by money. His love of Mother Nature impressed me, he cared deeply about the earth and mankind.

I started viewing my Mother Earth with more respect.

CHAPTER 46

What A Ride It Became

I ASKED TOM WHAT HE saw in me that he liked. He said I was intelligent, and I knew where I was going. He also said that I had such a sweetness about me. That made me feel perfect inside. He was so different from my other relationships. He was a free thinker and straightforward. Standing up for his beliefs, and not being afraid to stand behind them. He was uncomfortable holding hands or displaying any public affection. Ronny had always been so protective of me. He was not afraid to let the world know that he loved me. Ronny always held my hand. This was a big adjustment for me. I was from a family of no verbal or physical affection. I could do it easily. I had learned how to adapt to this kind of lifestyle.

Right after I met Tom and we started living together, he told me of his fear of being drafted into the military. He was not going to fight in the Vietnam War. I knew that he would never be able to survive that war, and he knew it too.

As it was nearing the end of the '60s, Peace Love and Rock and Roll was our mantra. We embraced it like no other generation had ever embraced their time in history before. We were proud to be hippies and flaunted it with our long hair. I embraced not wearing a bra or makeup. We loved one another, smoked pot, and loved music. We went to concerts and listened to a lot of live music. I feel that we were so fortunate to live in the sixties. It was the best time to experience such brilliant, real music. It was the era of the pure life we had loved so dearly. So much freedom and so many possibilities for a shift of peace on earth. Trust was something you expected from your friends. We all helped each other out and enjoyed spending time together.

Tom's best friend was planning a gold mining excursion. It was going to be a summer-long adventure, and he invited Tom to come along with him. Since it was the beginning of our relationship, he wanted me to come with them on the trip. Some of the other friends that were going did not wish to have any girls on this adventure. It was a little bit of a struggle between them to allow me to go. The parents wanted it to be an all-boys trip. After much negotiating between the parents, they decided to let me, and my friend Karen go on the journey with them. I gladly quit my job at the phone company. My friend Susie wanted to stay in my apartment while we were gone. She said she would pay the rent while we were gone for the summer. I did not want to lose my great place while we were gone, I agreed she could sublease it.

It was quite an adventure. We hiked down this beautiful trail that was so steep and scary. We had backpacks on to carry all our belongings. Karen and I also were responsible for carrying the trail mix. It was a large bag that was intended for all of us to share during our entire trip.

The guys packed in the dredge and all the gold mining supplies, sleeping bags, camp supplies, and all other necessities. Everything we needed for our gold mining adventure on the river that summer was carried by them. Well, those backpacks that we were carrying started getting extremely heavy to Karen and me. Even the trail mix seemed so heavy while we were hiking down to the river.

here comes
the
feeling you
thought
you'd forgotten

CHAPTER 47

Looking For Gold

As KAREN AND I WERE hiking we got hot, the bugs started biting, and we were getting hungry. We were walking ahead of the boys. We decided that if we just dropped some of the items out of our backpacks, it would make our hike a lot easier. Our packs would be lighter. We figured that they would find the stuff we dropped along the trail, pick them up and be happy to carry them for us. We also got hungry, so we decided to eat some of the trail mix. Well, the trail mix was supposed to be for the entire summer, and we pretty much had it all eaten by the time we got to the bottom of the trail. It didn't seem like we had eaten the whole supply, but it was gone. This would not be very well received by our fellow campmates. The boys finally all got down to the bottom of the trail with all the equipment. They were so hot and exhausted. They had been looking forward to the trail mix. We told them we had eaten almost all the trail mix. This wasn't what they wanted to hear, and they were angry. They were also mad about picking up our stuff along the way. They had about five thousand pounds of equipment with them. We only had to carry the trail mix and our clothes. Maybe they were not as good natured as we thought. Neither one of us had ever even been on a hike. We certainly had never backpacked. For all we knew there would be a cute rustic market at the end of the trail.

We were off to a great start. This is probably why the men did not want girls with them. They got over it quickly after we apologized.

Our gold mining adventure began on the river. We all helped set up camp. The men were very eager to start searching for the gold. There were fantasies of the gold rush all over again. They would find so much gold that they probably would not be able to carry it all up to the top of the trail. So much gold they would leave all the equipment there and just buy new stuff. They each started seeking out places to commence gold mining.

Karen and I stayed back at camp and got straight to work on our tans. We laid out in the sun and swam in the water all day. Then these ladybugs started to appear, and I was so excited to see them. The bugs began biting us, and I began to see red! My experience with ladybugs before had never included biting. It became my mission every day to dig holes in the dirt for my enemies. I would catch the ladybugs and put them in the hole, then I covered the top of the hole with leaves so they couldn't get out and bite me anymore. They would be set free in the evening.

I did feel guilty about that, but I did not like getting bit by the bugs.

CHAPTER 48

The Fish Tale

THE ONLY FOOD EXCEPT THAT delicious trail mix, that we had brought was dehydrated. Since we were not initially included in the planning stages, they really did not buy enough food for the extra two girls. We all had to ration the food, there definitely was not enough to go around. Everybody was getting hungry, and tempers started to flare a little bit. The guys were working hard mining all day. They were burning up a lot of energy, and they were getting weak. We had met this man at the bottom of the trail. He was so lovely, and he had the only cabin for as far as the eye could see. He was just a great guy. He was excited to see people there. He said no hikers had been down there in an incredibly long time. One day when the boys were out gold mining, he showed up at our campsite. He said he was going fishing. We asked if we could come along with him and he said he would love our company.

We had been trying to catch fish for about a month now. We did not have fishing poles or bait. None of us had caught any fish that were worthy of dinner. However, when this man threw his line in the river, he caught fish after fish after fish. He saw that we were famished, and we were unable to find any fish. He generously gave Karen and I both a full stringer of fish. As quickly as he arrived, he was gone. We were jumping for joy at our good fortune. We were so excited to have the fish. When the boys got back, we had told him that we had caught the fish ourselves.

I knew how to clean them, so they were ready to grill. We were providing dinner for our men to honor all their hard work. They were so surprised and grateful. We could say we had gained new respect at the camp. For that moment, they were happy to have us there. We lied to them and we did not catch that fish. The only thing we had caught was a stroke of great luck. It came in the form of this generous man. He had given us all these fish for dinner. For the first time since we had arrived at the river, we all had a full belly that night, and it felt good. Karen and I almost believed we really did catch the fish by the end of the night. The next day when they left to go mining, they said they were looking forward to seeing how many fish we would catch for dinner again. Fear consumed me. I had lied, and I had to catch fish for real. At the end of the day, the miners returned looking forward to another fish dinner. It was not there.

I had to confess my fish tale from the day before was just that, a fish tale.

CHAPTER 49

Is This The End?

THE NEXT MORNING WHEN WE woke up, there were a couple of guys who showed up with a big dog. They asked us if we feared staying at this remote campsite. There had been several stories in the news that someone was going around and killing campers in their sleeping bags. It was near the area that we were camping in. We did not know anything about this because we hadn't heard any news since we had been camping. Then I started thinking, are these the killers? Are they letting us know they're going to kill us? They decided to scout around the area and left the dog at our site. As if I wasn't uncomfortable enough with these visitors, their big dog decided he liked me. He started humping on my legs, and he wouldn't stop. My legs were bleeding. He basically was having his way with me. He wouldn't leave me alone. Everyone was afraid of trying to get the dog to leave me alone, and they were ready to go mining.

I started walking towards the water in hopes of losing that beast. I climbed up on a big rock out in the middle of the river. He swam out to where I was perched. He couldn't climb up to the top of the rock from the water. I sat out there for hours. He patiently waited for me to come down. I wasn't coming down. Finally, the owners returned and retrieved their dog. Shortly after that they left our campsite. This was the scariest four hours of my life on the river. I thought to myself, I have just been through so much in my lifetime there's no way that it is going to end like this. This was my time to be happy. I wasn't sure if they were the campground killers or if their dog would harm me. My legs were bloody from the dog's nails. I was so happy to see them go.

After three months, our gold mining adventure had come to an end. We were out of food and had not found too much gold. We broke down camp and started to prepare for the long, arduous hike out which was straight uphill. This was something Karen, and I dreaded. For some reason, that nice man showed up again at just the right time. He had driven his four-wheel-drive vehicle down to our site to check on us. He offered to drive Karen, and I back up the steep trail. He only had room for a couple of people. He put the gold dredging equipment on the back, and we quickly got in the front seat. He drove us up to his cabin while we waited for the others. When we arrived there, he gave us a can of Coca Cola and a can of tuna. I have never eaten anything so fast in all my life. I was starved. That Coke was the best one I had ever had. I have never been that skinny before nor after. The men arrived a few hours later, and we all hiked back to our cars. This was such a fantastic once in a lifetime experience. I will never forget it and my first one with my new boyfriend, Tom. I learned from that trip several life lessons. The time spent is all about how it turns out in the end. All the things in between are just part of the journey.

On our first day back to civilization we went and visited a friend that lived very close to where we had been on the river. We were very excited for our first dinner. We went to the market and bought some pork ribs. We had big plans to have a barbecue at his house. We had not had anything to eat except dehydrated food and a few fish for over three months. Don't forget we ate all the trail mix too on the first day. We were drooling for those ribs! We cooked those ribs and gobbled them up lickety-split. Maybe an hour later I started getting so sick. I was not in tune with my body that well. I really had to learn a lot of things from my experiences. I had never been taught life's most simple skills. Looking back, it was so stupid. Don't eat pork ribs after you have not had anything substantial to eat for three months. Start out with something light and work your way up. I learned that sitting on the toilet while vomiting in the sink. That went on for about a week. I was so happy when I started feeling better. Slow and easy wins the race.

Food is not leaving the planet. You can have some more tomorrow. Don't eat all the trail mix in one day.

Reflection

I JUST WANT TO REFLECT for just a moment.......

When I say "looking back" I want to add this. If you have one foot in the past and one foot in the future...you are just pissing on today! I don't want to waste any moments of time today. I want to use all sixty seconds of that minute wisely. I want to live in the moment. When I look at the forest, I want to see the trees. Then I want to see the branches and the leaves. Then I want to see the insects and birds in the trees. I want to feel the wind or rain in the trees. I want to see the sunlight in the forest and the trees. I want to watch it long enough to look at the changes in the colors and the shadows as the sun goes down. I want to see it at night with all the stars outshining on it. I want to look at the full moon shining on it. I want to hear the animals moving around and rustling through the leaves. I want to see the sky and see the clouds. I want to imagine all the different things that I see in the shapes of clouds. I want to see and feel the silver linings that I see in the clouds. In other words, I always want to experience my seven senses to the best of my ability.

I cannot have regrets. If I would have done things differently, I can only imagine all the different mistakes I could have made. Instead, I want to think about how I lived in the moment. How did I feel when that was going on? What was the lesson I learned? I cannot look back through sixty-six-year-old eyes and judge what

I did when I was two years old. I didn't know then what I do now. It's only because of the many mistakes I made in my life that I have learned so many beautiful things. I know I am smarter. Of course, I would have walked better at sixteen months old if I just knew how to do it. I learned how to do it by falling and getting back up again.

I am pretty good at it now. But I am not mad at myself for not doing a better job at sixteen months old.

I have grown tired of the battles in my own head. "What if's" especially are painful, unless your "what if's" are glorious. That is why I say live in your moment and appreciate who you are at that moment. Don't be judgmental about anything. Everyone is doing the best they can with what they know. Everyone has a story. Lay your weapons down inside yourself. Be at peace in your own heart. Keep everything around you peaceful and beautiful.

CHAPTER 51

I'm Back

BACK TO MY LIFE BEFORE I became enlightened.

We made our journey back home. We spent many nights camping out along the way. It was an adventure that I would never forget or ever regret. When I arrived back at my hometown, I expected my friend to let me move back into my apartment. After all, that was the agreement we had made before I left. She loved it there and said she was not going to move out. This was quite a surprise to me. With this unexpected turn of events, we ended up sleeping in the back of our truck. We had not worked all summer, and that meant we had not earned any money either. Tom moved back home, and I went to stay with my aunt.

My aunt told me where my biological Father was.

I got in contact with him again. I went to visit him, and he was living with my cousin. I asked if I could stay with them until I was able to get back on my feet. Tom came to pick me up one day, and he met my Father. He told Tom that when he dies, he could look him up in hell. He will be the one selling speed. I remember thinking who would say that to my boyfriend? One day when I was alone with my cousin, he told me he wanted to have sex with me. I said NO! He said that my father had told him to have sex with me or my Father would have to rape me. I found out that my Mom had put him in jail for not paying child support to her. He was angry about it and had a lot of resentment towards me. My own Father wanted me to pay for it.

I left immediately. I went back a few days later to retrieve my belongings, but they were all gone. I never saw either of them again.

It was then that I realized I was lucky not to have my Father as a role model when I was growing up. My parents showed me everything morally, and emotionally that I did not want to be. The only thing that either of them ever gave me was life, during a one-night stand. My Mom had told me many times that I had ruined her life. My Father resented me for having to spend time in jail for not paying child support. This does not create very good self esteem. I quickly put that all out of my mind.

I did not want to follow in my parents footsteps and I did not have to. I can be the person I want to be. I don't want to drink, take drugs, steal, be irresponsible, out of control and unloving. I want to make my own mistakes, not theirs.

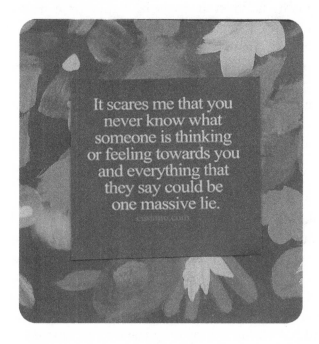

CHAPTER 52

One Door Closes

Tom & I found another place to live together. I easily found employment working at a car dealership. It was fun, and I enjoyed working there. I was offered more money by another dealership that was across the street. I gave my notice and went to work at another dealership. I really liked working there also. One of the girls I was working with, and I became best friends. I loved going to work. One day at the close of the day I was called into my manager's office. He asked me if I wanted to go to the roof with him to see the sunset. I said sure, I did not know at the time he was a pig. He pulled down a ladder to the roof. I had on a skirt, and he told me to climb up first. I was uncomfortable and very naive. It was a beautiful view. We watched the sunset and came back down the ladder to the office. He offered me a raise in pay for the outstanding work that I was performing. I thought it was for doing a good job, but it wasn't. He wanted me to have sex with him in exchange for more money every month. I told him there was not any amount of money no matter how much it was, that could be worth having to do that. I went home crying and told Tom. I questioned myself again. What had I done to provoke this? He said you don't have to go back to work. I was worried about not having a paycheck to pay the rent.

I felt uncomfortable and I knew it was wrong. I needed to trust it would go the right way if I did too.

CHAPTER 53

Another One Opens

I TOOK A CHANCE, AND I quit. I found another job very quickly. I was offered more money, and it was closer to home.

I started working for a nice older gentleman. His wife worked in the office, and he wanted her to stay at home. He put me in charge of overseeing the entire office. He paid me a very nice salary, and we had a lovely rapport. With the increase in my wages, we were able to move to the beach. I was in heaven with a great job and a cute cottage at the beach. I have always been so comfortable on the ocean. I love beachcombing, swimming, body surfing, fishing, playing with my dogs, and having friends over for barbecues. Life was going my way, and I enjoyed it!

My youngest brother came to live with us. He was ten years old, and my Mom wanted him out of her house. Our beach cottage was a tiny little place. One of Tom's co-workers needed a place to live. He could help us with the rent. He had just moved to California from Wyoming, and he had never been in the ocean. It was fun to have him around while he explored all that our state had to offer. Sadly, we sent my brother back home. My mom wanted him to stay, but we needed the extra money. She had never offered to contribute anything. She expected me to take responsibility for him. My brother did not want to leave. Once again I had let him down. I felt horrible about it. I was doing the best I could.

I felt she could trash her life but I did not want her to trash and control mine.

CHAPTER 54

Make Love Not War

THE VIETNAM WAR WAS GOING strong. Several of our friends had already been drafted. Many of them regretfully did not make it home. The government started the lottery to fulfill their draft quotas. Tom was a true pacifist, and he stated that on his draft application. I can remember with great anxiety turning on our black and white tv to watch the first numbers being drawn for the lottery. They called out birth dates instead of numbers. It did not take long for his birthday to be called, he was the 56th number that was chosen. He was drafted immediately, and he knew he couldn't go. His priest, employers, and friends all wrote letters to the draft board expressing their sentiments that he would never survive. He was a true conscientious objector. Everyone that knew him was confident he could not pick up a gun and kill. The draft board ignored his consciousness objector beliefs and drafted him. They gave him a date to report for his induction, and he did not go. He was officially on the run.

I had Friday afternoons off at work. One Friday morning I was getting ready to go to work. I made Tom breakfast and began preparing his lunch before I left for work. He told me not to make him lunch as he was not up to going to work because he did not feel well. I called his job and let them know that he was ill and he wouldn't be coming to work. I came home at noon. I checked on him, and he was still sleeping. I put on my bathing suit and went out with my neighborhood friend to lay on our boat dock to soak up the sun. After a while, I started to get thirsty. I asked my friend if she would like some lemonade. She said she would. I went upstairs to make some ice-cold drinks for us. As I was walking out the door with the fresh lemonade, the phone rang.

I did not want the ringing phone to wake up Tom, so I put the drinks down and answered the phone. It was Tom's work. His boss was on the other end of the line. He wanted to speak to Tom. I was surprised because he had never called before. I told him he was asleep and not feeling well. He told me that the FBI had just been out at the company looking for Tom. They told the FBI that he had called in sick and wasn't there. He just wanted to warn him. I thanked him and hung up the phone. I went into the bedroom and woke up Tom and told him about the conversation I just had with his boss. We lived on an island in Sunset Beach. You had to drive over a bridge to get to our house. Tom got out of bed and looked out the window. He saw the FBI car coming over the bridge right at that very moment. He ran downstairs and got into a dingy we had tied to the dock. I was still in shock in the kitchen. He told my friend that was waiting for me to bring back the lemonade, that the FBI was there looking for him. My friend hopped in the boat and escaped with him. They rowed the boat around the back of the canal to her house. I looked out the window to see the FBI park the car right in front of the garage. They jumped out of their car and ran up our stairs to catch him. I answered the door in my bathing suit holding the lemonade. They flashed their badges and told me they were looking for Tom Breslin. I told them he wasn't there. They pushed their way into the apartment and started searching for him in our small place. It took them only minutes to discover that he was not there. They said they knew he lived there because they saw his fishing box in the closet. I asked how they knew it was his and they said it had the name Tom painted on it. I said "yes" he does live here. Because Tom had siblings, he always put his name on everything. I always thought it was funny how he labeled all his belongings. Tom still does label his stuff. They wanted to know where he was. They let me know they could arrest me for harboring a fugitive if I didn't tell them everything. I was scared but I felt this was very typical of things I had seen in movies when the FBI gets their man.

I offered them some lemonade and tried to make them feel comfortable. They asked me if I was one of those hippie girls that ate granola, smoked pot and was all natural and stuff. I asked them if they were mormon and I noticed their shiny shoes. I found it funny that we were trading first impressions with each other.

The phone rang right after they had arrived. It was from my neighborhood friend. I thought to myself I bet she is still waiting on the dock for me and her lemonade. She asked me if I had some company? I said "yes." She said "So do I". I then knew where Tom was, he was at her house watching the FBI through binoculars from across the street at her house. I hung up and they wanted to know who it was. The phone rang again. They told me they really did not want me to answer the phone again. I told them it might be Tom. They let me answer the phone. It was a childhood neighbor friend of Tom's. He said that the FBI had been in the neighborhood looking for Tom. Everyone knew Tom was a draft resistor and they supported his decision. They had told me they were going to stay there and wait for him to come home. I hung up the phone and told the men that several people knew what was going on because they had been contacted by the FBI. I said Tom would probably not be coming home now. They asked me why I thought that? I told them because your car is parked right in front of our garage. They looked at each other, and one of them said he would go down and move the vehicle. He went and moved the car and then came back upstairs. I asked them if they were going to spend the night? I could get some bedding out for them to be comfortable. I offered them the couch. They arrived around one p.m. and it was now after six o'clock. After the traffic had died down, they decided to head on home. They gave me their card and instructed me to call them immediately after I talked to him.

I quickly had become his caregiver without ever even knowing it.

CHAPTER 55

History In The Making

I CALLED TOM TO LET him know they were gone. He called his priest. He put him in touch with another priest at Oxford college. The priest told him to come to Oxnard and stay with him. He packed an overnight bag and headed to the college. They were sympathetic to the Vietnam war conscientious objectors. The priest called a lawyer that was a friend of his. He explained to him that he had a conscientious objector that did not show up for his military draft service. He had been denied this status and refused to be inducted into the military. He needed help and he did not have any money to hire an attorney. Mr. Shapiro agreed to help him and told him not to worry about the money. He then notified the F.B.I. and told them that he had Tom in his custody and would be delivering him to the courthouse the next morning. For the first time in years, Tom was able to rest easy and get a good night's sleep.

Tom and I met Mr. Shapiro the next morning in his Beverly Hills office. We then drove to the courthouse. When we arrived I looked around at all of the people on the courthouse steps. In the crowd, I saw some historical icon figures. First I saw Daniel Ellsberg. He had just uncovered the pentagon papers. Angela Davis with her huge afro hairstyle was the next one I saw. An American political activist. She was beautiful. It gave me so much hope to be living in this era. I felt we really were going to make a change.

We then went into the Los Angeles Count detention area. Mr. Shapiro turned Tom in just as he told the F.B.I he would. The courts said he could be released if we could post $250.00 for his bail. That might as well have been a million dollars to us. We did not have that kind of money. I called Tom's mom and explained what had happened. I asked her if she could come down to the court and post his $250.00 bail. I promised we would pay her back as soon as we could. She said yes and she came right away.

Tom was released and we went home in our little brown VW. Life went on as usual while we waited for the courts to pick a trial date. I will never forget the kindness of the priest that secured that lawyer for Tom. Mr. Shapiro was the kindest, compassionate and generous man. He was dedicated to draft resistors and conscientious objectors. We were so fortunate to have him on our side. The judge that conducted the trial was a new judge, and no one really knew what his stand would be on draft dodgers.

Tom cut his long hair and put on some mainstream clothing and off to meet his fate he went. The judge sentenced him to two years of alternative service and three years of probation. We were so relieved. I can remember driving home from work that night and being so excited to see Tom. When I arrived on my street, I looked up, and he was at the window smiling. His hair was short. He looked happy. No more sleepless nights. No more looking over his shoulder.

He started working in a hospital to serve his alternative service sentence. He would always say that if he didn't go to war to kill people, they wanted him to watch them die in the hospital. I had always wanted Tom to turn himself in so that he could start living his life freely. He did not agree with me and held onto his convictions about doing things his way. I quickly learned to respect that. You cannot want something for someone more than they want it for themselves. It bears repeating and remembering. The only thing you can do is to love and embrace them.

Tom has always been very good with his hands. He got a job working at another hospital in the Carpentry Department. Tom was training with a carpenter that had come to America from Germany. He learned a lot about being a master craftsman from him. Several of the doctors from the hospital asked him to do some carpentry on their personal houses. He was enjoying his new occupation and making some money on the side. One day when he was at work he and his mentor got into a fight. The co-worker had quite a temper and threw his hammer at Tom. Tom threw his hammer back at him. He yelled out and told him he was fired. Tom went up to human resources, and he quit. He had served his two years that he was required to do by his sentence from the government. After he resigned, he went over to his friend Gary's house. They had been friends for a very long time.

Tom always thought of himself first. I should have learned from that.

CHAPTER 56

Peace Begets Peace

WHILE THEY WERE HAVING A beer, his friend said to him "Hey I'm going to Alaska tomorrow do you want to come with me?" Tom said, "I just quit my job and my two years of alternative service is over so yeah let's go." He called me from Gary's house, and he told me that he had left his job. He then proceeded to tell me that he was going to Alaska with his friend the next day. I said to him does this mean that we are breaking up? He said he wasn't sure at that moment what was going to be happening, but he was on his way home, and we could talk about it. I could help him pack. I helped him pack, and he was off to Alaska the next day. I really wasn't sure what this all meant. All I knew for sure was that I was alone and needed to handle everything by myself. Once again, my past had served me well. I knew how to take care of myself at twenty-one years old. I was confident that I could handle this. Tom had not contributed to much financially because of his draft situation and I knew I could figure it out.

I carried on with my life. I went to work and played with my friends. I joined the ERA organization. The Equal Rights Amendment (ERA) is a proposed amendment to the United States Constitution designed to guarantee equal legal rights for all American citizens regardless of sex.

At one of the meetings I bought a POW MIA Vietnam Bracelet. Prisoner of War Missing in Action Bracelet. I went to the meetings and I was actively protesting the capture of our soldiers.

I was living a pretty happy life. Living at the beach, being alone for the first time. One day when I came home from work I found a card on my door. It said "Tom, please call me." The card was from his probation officer. What a shock, he had never contacted Tom once in the two years he was serving his alternative service.

Now that Tom was gone, he wanted to check in with him. I called his probation officer and let him know Tom had gone to Alaska. He was angry. I had no idea that he was not allowed to leave the state for the next one year without his permission. His officer let me know what was up.

I called Tom and let him know that he had broken the law, and his probation officer was mad! Tom reported to the United States Federal Building in Anchorage. He was assigned a very understanding probation officer. He was very sympathetic to Vietnam War Objectors. He took down all the pertinent information that he needed and told him not to worry about anything. He felt that he had not done anything wrong and he would take care of it. It was taken care of, and that was that. The officer told Tom he was all clear and he never needed to see him again, as long as he stayed out of trouble.

About three years later Tom received a letter from the President of the United States. He anxiously opened his mail and found a Presidential Pardon. President Gerald Ford had issued pardons to some of the conscientious objectors that he felt were sincere. He had only issued about 2500 pardons. He did not grant them to deserters or draft dodgers. Tom was fortunate to receive one.

We have that pardon framed and hanging in a prominent place in the house to this day. I could spend a lot of time talking about this subject. It was so near and dear to me, and I still feel a lot of emotions about it. I felt the ones who went to Vietnam had a lot of courage. I felt the ones who stood up and said they could not do it had a lot of courage. Some people just do not have it in them to kill living things. I have the same respect for both. Both of them were brave. I cry and pray for both. I was so grateful when one of our friends would come home safely. I was especially happy when my friend Patches returned. I had so much relief when I saw him. He was a gentle soul and I worried about him. To this day there has never been a gun or weapon in our house. I do feel very grateful to those that can fight for our country, and I pray for them. All young men and women must do what their heart tells them to do.

I also believe that peace begets peace.

CHAPTER 57

Life's A Beach

I stayed in my little beach house for about 6 more months. While I was alone I would often think about Ronny and wonder if he was happy. I still really missed him. Tom finally called and asked me to join him. I gathered and packed all of my things. I decided what I could live without and had a garage sale! For some reason, my mom had found out that I was moving and selling all of my things. Suddenly, she showed up at my home. It was about eight o'clock in the morning, and she was already drunk. I had not seen her in six years. My friend Jean was there with me helping me to pack. My drunken mother and calling her my name because she thought she was me. "Gee mom so glad to see you, I am over here" was running through my mind. I thought for a moment that I hoped she wouldn't hit her, but at least I am safe. My mom went into the garage to gather the things of mine that she wanted. She got a lot of stuff and handed me $5.00 for all of it. That was the last time I ever saw her. I guess you could say I started to finally feel that she would not be able to hurt me anymore. I think that was the reason I was eager to trade in the beach for the snow. That thought made Alaska feel safe for me. It is a terrible feeling to always be afraid of someone coming to beat you. You never really get a good night's sleep. You tend to assess every situation and wonder if you will be ambushed or safe. When you walk into a room you start checking everything out carefully. You are looking for things that may hurt you. I still do it to this day. I analyze the situation and sum it up very quickly. I was never really at ease. I was still very afraid of what she may come and do to me. Those feelings were real no matter how hard I tried to ignore them and pretend that life was great.

I am always aware that there is a possibility of a dangerous situation. I look for the good and embrace that instead of evil. I always know thou art with me. I am acutely aware of predators, and I am not easy prey for them. I have already lived with that kind of fear. That is another good thing about getting all the bad stuff over with early on. It makes you such a strong person for the rest of your life. Everything happens for a reason. The fear that overcame me when I saw my mom drive up was quickly replaced by the confidence that she could not hurt me anymore. Those days of her control over me were becoming very distant.

Remember that it is always up to you what kind of day you have.

CHAPTER 58

The Other Mother

TOM'S MOTHER WAS NOT FOND of me. I came from the wrong side of the tracks. My family was not flush with money, and I was not Catholic. What kind of a girl doesn't have a relationship with her own mother she had asked her son? Tom and I lived together in sin. She was a devout Catholic. In fact, the only redeeming quality she saw in me was that I had straight teeth. His mom was very vocal about her dislike of me. Our first Thanksgiving together as a couple she invited Tom for dinner but not me. He asked if I was included in that invitation and she quickly said no. He responded that if I weren't invited, he would not be coming to dinner. I felt so much respect for him standing up for me.

She did reluctantly invite me over when I was ready for my journey to join Tom in Alaska. I brought my two dogs with me to her home. I was going to have dinner and say goodbye to his family. She made me put the dogs in the backyard. They rubbed their noses on the window to see where I was. During dinner, she said to me that she hoped I was planning on taking a day off work before I moved to come over and wash her windows. The dog's noses pressed against her windows were a big problem. It upset me so much that I just got up and excused myself from the table and left her home. This was very unusual for me because I usually would do the dishes and clean her kitchen before I went home. I was used to being made to feel like I was expected to do the chores.

I was expected to perform these duties while the family sat in the living room and relaxed. I know it may seem silly now looking back on it. I was already sensitive and nervous, this just pushed me over the edge. I began to feel that I was less than them and I did not deserve to be treated as such. I had supported and loved her son and it was ignored because I wasn't a member of her church. I did not come from their neighborhood. I was a girl who had survived a bad situation. Instead of feeling sorry for myself I felt good about myself. I did not find excuses, I looked for solutions. I did not reach out for drugs and alcohol. I dug deep inside myself and found strength. I saw the results of addiction and I wanted nothing to do with it. I was better than that. I am stronger than that.

CHAPTER 59

Stressed Out

I BURST INTO TEARS AND drove to my friend Lana's house. I was so upset. I started itching all over my body. She thought if I took a bath at her home, I might get some relief. She came in and saw my back while I was in the bathtub. I had welts the size of small pancakes all over my body. The next morning, I went to the doctors because the bumps were still there. They itched like crazy. The doctor said I had hives that were probably caused by stress. He gave me a prescription for phenobarbital for relief. I took one pill when I got home, and I slept for two days. I slept through the entire next day, and I missed going to work. Friends were calling to check on me and I never even heard the phone ring.

This was the first time that I had stood up for myself. I was terrified to do it. I just felt like I was getting tired of being the lame duck. My body reacted to my stress level. I think leaving for Alaska made me feel like no one could find me there. It was far enough away that I felt secure. I never looked back, and I was moving on. I had survived his mom and mine! The victory was mine, I felt strong. I realized it was their problem that they did not like me, not mine. It felt good.

Tom's sister had decided she would like to drive with me to Alaska. I was happy to have the company. I packed all my belongings into my car with my two dogs and went to pick her up at his mom's house. She said she would be ready at 10:00 p.m. We would then depart on my new adventure. I got there about ten minutes early and knocked on the door. Tom's mom came to the door and said his sister wasn't there. She told me I could wait in the garage for her and slammed the door in my face. It was cold in the garage.

I just couldn't help but think how warm and cozy it must have been inside. It sure would be nice to take a little nap while I was waiting for her. A cup of hot tea would be very yummy. The longer I waited for her, the more hurt I became. She didn't get home until after two a.m. She said, "let me get my stuff and tell my mom goodbye, and we will be on our way." I waited in the car. She finally came out and said her mom wanted me to come in and say goodbye. I looked at her and said, "tell her I said goodbye." I had no desire to go into that house ever again. I was so hurt. I had never done anything to her but be nice. I loved her son and took good care of him. I remember thinking about what a massive waste of time it was, sitting in that cold, dark garage. I didn't even get an apology from his sister for being four hours late. I could have been

I could have been 250 miles away by now.

What a memorable send-off. Not the one I hoped for, but it was memorable. I took a deep breath with my eye on the prize.

Not everyone likes me and that's fine with me. In fact I do not like everyone either. She was the one missing out. I had a lot of love to give and if she didn't want it there are others that do.

CHAPTER 60

Road Trip

OFF WE WENT, DRIVING TO Oregon to stay at Tom's brother's house. While we were there, his sister found a nice VW camping bus for sale. Her brother agreed to buy it for her. She couldn't wait to get back home as soon as possible and show it off. That left me driving to Alaska by myself. I was twenty-one years old. I was glad I was so capable of caring for myself. I couldn't believe my bad luck getting into such a selfish family. Did I do this on purpose? I really wanted a loving, caring family. At this point, I thought I am not meant to be truly loved ever. They were not physically abusive like my family, just cold and they did not like me. Once again, I did not fit in. I am beginning to realize I am different. Off I went with a smile on my face determined to make the journey. Not my problem and I will not be seeing them anytime soon. They did not appreciate me or the love I had to give. The fact that they were not able to receive any love from me made me feel so sad.

I stayed in some campgrounds along the way if the weather permitted. One night while I was settling in for the night a guy stopped by my camping site to say hello. My dog went crazy, barking and growling. I believe she sensed that the stranger was up to no good. I told him he should be moving along. I didn't know what my dog might do to him. He scurried off. He wasn't willing to stick around to see what might happen. I felt very safe after that. I continued to camp out along the way for about two more weeks.

When I got up to Seattle, I put my car on the ferry. I boarded the plane with my two dogs in carriers. It was official and sort of surreal I was on my way to Anchorage. I put on my down jacket and closed-toe shoes. For the first time in my life I did not have on flip-flops. I was excited and apprehensive all at the same time.

Tom was very excited to see me when we landed. It had been six months since we had seen each other. He was living in Girdwood which was about an hour from the airport. I can remember landing in Anchorage and looking out of the plane window. There was so much snow everywhere. My mind wandered back to the mud snowballs that I had handcrafted in my backyard. I wondered what the heck was I doing here? The beach fed my soul. I loved walking on the beach every night. The sunsets, swimming, beachcombing, surf fishing, getting tan, riding bikes and our Catamaran Sailing Boat. I would miss the energy of the water and the sand. I was not so sure I had made the best decision. I felt comfort in being so far away from any family. I was excited about the new horizon and all the potential possibilities. What exciting people would I meet? What were native Eskimos like? Would I meet them? What kind of job would I get? Who would be my first new friend I would encounter? Would there be wild animals all around the city? I was about to find out! My sense of adventure that had been cultivated as a young child was serving me well. I was not afraid to be in a new environment.

I was excited at all of the new experiences I would have. I knew I would trust my instincts and live the life I was born to live.

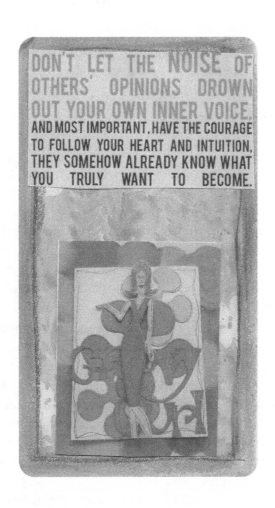

DON'T LET THE NOISE OF OTHERS' OPINIONS DROWN OUT YOUR OWN INNER VOICE. AND MOST IMPORTANT, HAVE THE COURAGE TO FOLLOW YOUR HEART AND INTUITION, THEY SOMEHOW ALREADY KNOW WHAT YOU TRULY WANT TO BECOME.

CHAPTER 61

Our First Night

OUR TWO DOGS, TOM & I started out driving to his home in Girdwood. It was about an hour's drive from the airport in Anchorage. Driving down the highway with snow and ice all around me was a sight that I had never experienced before. It was awesome. The sky was so dark without city lights to brighten it. We finally got to the house and we were excited to get inside and warm up. When we started to go through the door, it seemed to be taking a long time to get inside. Tom discovered that he had lost the keys to the house. Are you kidding me? It was freezing cold outside, and I was shivering. After looking for quite some time he could not find them. He finally decided to break a window. He crawled in through the window to unlock the door and we finally got in. It was about 25 degrees. Even the dogs were cold, and they had a lot of fur on them. I suddenly knew what the three-dog night expression was all about. You need to sleep with that many just to keep you warm. Happy to see each other we all settled in for a long winter's night.

So many ways I need to learn to adapt in this new state. Am I strong enough?

CHAPTER 62

The Land Of The Midnight Sun

A FEW DAYS LATER MY car arrived on the ferry. We took the drive to Anchorage to get the car. As soon as I retrieved it, I called the local car dealership to get it winterized. For some reason, the owner of the dealership had answered my phone call. As I was making my appointment for service, I told him I had worked in a car dealership in California. I had just moved to Alaska and needed to prepare my car for winter driving. He gave me an impromptu interview over the phone and offered me a job. I started working the next day. Seriously could it really be that easy? I got my car winterized, and he got a new employee.

We started looking for a home in Anchorage to rent. It was near impossible to find any rentals available. The Valdez pipeline was in full swing of being built. It seemed as if every oilman in the United States was living there. We would wait at the newspaper stand for the paper to come out. We would grab out the want ads and look for places to rent and call the numbers immediately. There was so few rental properties are available. It was like a big lottery game. How fast could you get the paper, scan the want ads and then run to the payphone and plead your case to the potential landlord? We finally found one after doing the same routine for about three weeks. We rented it sight unseen. It turned out to be quite a dump. It was very close to being inhabitable. I just thought about how much better I could make it look. We could paint it, make some curtains, buy some new rugs to make it more like home. This house was freezing cold. No matter how much heat you put into it, it would not warm up. We stayed there for less than a month. We had gone to bed one night and started to feel snow and water dripping on our faces. The entire roof was collapsing. Luckily, we got out before it collapsed on us and we were not hurt. We moved out that night and went to a hotel. The search was on again.

One of my dogs hated the cold. Bandit did not even like to go outside to go to the bathroom. He would step in the snow, lift his paw up out of the snow and shake it off. He put the next leg in and shook it off like crazy. Poor thing he was so miserable. He missed the beach. I understood how he felt. I was missing the beach too. Living in the Alaskan wilderness was going to take some time to get used to.

At my new job, one of my coworkers was so kind to me. A couple of times per week I would walk down through the snow to the Lucky Wishbone hamburger and chicken restaurant near our office. I would get her lunch for her, and in return for the cold walk, she would pay for mine. I did it for her every week. I was so grateful to her for the opportunity to save money on my lunch. I told her about my poor dog, and she decided to take Bandit to live with her. She wanted an indoor lap dog. He was perfect for her and her husband. While out and about we would see them in their car driving around with Bandit riding on the top of their seats. They would go out to eat and buy him his own meal and bring it out for him to eat. I was so happy to see this. This family was so perfect for him. It was easier for us to find a place to live with just one dog too.

We finally found a cute little house to rent. It was on the street called Lovejoy what great energy it had! We had several roommates to help pay the rent. It was a lot of fun, and it was warm.

We only had one car and since I had never driven in the snow before Tom always took me to work and picked me up. One snowy day Tom decided I could drive the car myself to work. He dug the car out of the snow in the driveway. He gave me a push and off I went. I could see him waving goodbye to me in the rearview mirror. It went well until I got on the main highway which was about one block away. I stopped at the stoplight when it turned red. When it became green, I wasn't going anywhere. My wheels were merely spinning around. I looked ahead of me, and I saw a plane that was making an emergency landing right on the highway directly in front of me. I got so scared and thought that this would be my last day on earth. I was frozen in my tracks.

The plane landed just a few feet in front of my car. I got out of the car. I walked home crying hysterically. When I got back home, I walked through the door and threw the car keys at Tom. I told him if you want your car you can go get it in the middle of Northern Lights Blvd. I went into the bedroom sobbing. I packed my suitcase. I came out and said I am leaving, please take me to the airport. As soon as I grabbed my bag to leave, an earthquake started. Tom caught me and pushed me to a safe area. I was out of control. He told me to go lay down, go to sleep and he would go get the car. I cried myself to sleep. I stayed in Alaska, but I kept that suitcase packed and sitting by the front door for years. I was driven back & forth to work after that. I slowly learned how-to drive-in snow and ice. I started saving for a 4-wheel drive car.

Tom decided to become a union carpenter. He enrolled in the apprenticeship program. He recruited his best friend to join him and off they went to begin their new careers. It was a four-year program. I committed to working while he studied and completed his program. I remember buying him a handheld calculator for $39.00. I also hired a tutor for him because he was struggling with math. More than anything I wanted him to succeed. It did not come quickly to him, and he struggled with the math.

I need to stick it out and learn from this. Don't be a quitter.

CHAPTER 63

Where Am I And Why?

I WAS SO LONELY. I was desperate for friends. I did not know anyone except Tom's friend that he drove up with. I vividly remember my first visit to the bank to open a checking account. My first impression was WOW. There were taxidermy trophies of moose, bears, salmon and other wild animals all displayed on the walls. I freaked out! Never had I ever seen a stuffed wild animal let alone so many heads of animals. I tried to make friends with the girl who helped me to open my checking account. She was not interested but told me some places to meet people. I was so pathetic, and I felt so lonely. My husband was in school all day and studied all night. I had just turned twenty-one years old. I wanted to go out and experience the nightlife. I really could not relate to all these outdoor activities. Swimming and laying in the sun were my passion, not snow skiing. What was I thinking of moving here? I just remember thinking I will be away from the threats of my mother.

I found another job that paid more money. It was great. It was a company that managed the Native Corporation Properties. There were about twelve girls in my office. Each employee managed and did the bookkeeping for one property. The properties were spread out through Alaska, mostly in rural villages. I was so happy working there. My office was in a two-story brand-new building. When it snowed, it felt like I was in a snow globe. Very surreal and magical was the view. I volunteered to work any available extra hours. I eventually had five properties to manage. Most of the properties I was given to manage were hotels. I managed one local restaurant too. The managers of the properties would bring the paperwork etcetera to me. The restaurant manager always brought me hot french-fries! BONUS!! I met my new best friend there. She had just gotten divorced and was dating a carpenter. He eventually became her new husband. Quickly he became a supervisor of a sheetrock company. We went out together every weekend. Her husband and Tom got along great. We remain friends to this day. I became close to the owner of the corporation. He called me into his office one day and told me he would give me a raise if I would buy myself some new clothes. I agreed and went shopping. I showed up in a new dress the next day. Apparently, I looked much better dressed as a girl in a dress than the overalls and flannel shirts I had gotten used to.

He went on to become the governor. I remained loyal to him. He changed my Alaskan experience in a good way. I worked for him six days a week and at least ten hours per day. I made a lot of new friends. I started accumulating side jobs also. I went to school and became a tax accountant. My days were full, and I loved it. I was making significant money and made many new friends. It was time for a new CEO at Sheffield Enterprises. We had grown, and the owner wanted to pursue other government opportunities. The new CEO did not like all the power that he felt I had over the office's daily operation. He started to belittle me and question everything that I did. I knew what was coming. He wanted subservient workers. I was not any of the things he wanted in his new office. I had worked there when they just began, and I knew a lot about the ins and outs of the daily operations. I helped the auditors. We were under a lot of scrutiny because of the native corporations. We had full-time auditors watching every move we made. We also were getting our first computer system. This was a massive transition from doing hand entries. The computer was huge. There were so many changes so quickly.

I had started potluck lunches on Fridays when I first started working there. We would all bring a dish and enjoy lunch together. There were so many great cooks in the office. I still use many of the recipes that I got from those potlucks. The new CEO put a stop to that right away. He felt it took too much of our attention and it was a waste of time. We worked in a big open room. This was so fun to be able to help each other with situations that would arise daily. The stories we heard were so funny. For instance, one property was going through a ton of toilet paper. The reason being that the natives had never used toilet paper before. They loved it. They would drive their snowmobiles through corridors of the hotel and snag all the toilet paper from the rooms. Things like that made us all have a good laugh and then order more toilet paper for them.

The new CEO wanted all of us to have our own cubicles. There would be no more stories, no more helping each other. I was no longer able to go in and talk with the owner. The CEO wanted me to go through him for everything. I was used to being in control and uplifting the staff. Clearly, he wanted a different working environment. It was time for me to move on. I turned in my resignation. Nine out of the twelve girls that worked with me all quit too. Everything I wanted out of this job I received. It was a great place to meet new friends and feel a sense of family. I am still in touch with a lot of these folks.

I would have to say the lesson that I learned here is that there is a time and a reason for every season. We create situations to benefit our need for a particular amount of time. Once that has been fulfilled we must cultivate new chapters to our story.

CHAPTER 64

What's Next?

I DECIDED TO START SELLING cosmetics with an organization that focused on the door to door sales. I went knocking on doors to pass out catalogs and look for customers. I had several part-time jobs. I also started helping one of my friends that I had met in my previous employment. When she had quit her career along with me, she started a cleaning business. She cleaned several local bars. That was the most putrid smelling job I had ever had. When you turn the lights on in a bar, you would be shocked at what you would see. The only fun part was coming up with new drink ideas. After cleaning the bars in the early morning, I went back to selling my products. I knocked on a door while I was passing out catalogs and this charming girl about my age opened the door. She invited me in. We talked for quite a while. She placed a big order with me. She started telling me that her husband owned some grocery stores. He was looking for a new accountant. His business was growing, and he needed someone to help manage them all. She told him about me, and he set up an interview to meet me. I was living in Alaska when everything was busting loose. While the oil pipeline was being constructed money was abundant. It was not a female-friendly environment. Most girls stayed at home or they were exotic dancers. The world was my oyster. I sold cosmetics, did accounting jobs on the side, cleaned bars and now I got another new job. I was using my time wisely, and it was paying off. Tom was still in carpenter school as an apprentice.

I was building my own empire. I figured out I was smart and I could get things done. This was the perfect time for both of these skills.

CHAPTER 65

I Can Do This

MY FIRST DAY AT MY new job was quite an eye-opener. After one week I knew there was a lot of theft going on. My new boss gave me his check-register so I could enter all of the original transactions. There were not any computers, internet, cordless phones or fax machines invented yet. Everything was done by hand with plug-in calculators, pencils, paper and erasers. His bookkeeper showed a $20,000.00 balance in the bank. When I reconciled it with the bank statements, he was $12.00 overdrawn. He was so shocked that he didn't believe me. He went to the bank and reconciled it with them, and they confirmed it. Many of his employees were stealing everything. The bookkeeper was keeping the books so everything looked great. In reality he was in a lot of financial trouble. I went home crying my eyes out. I said to myself I am either going to quit and walk away from this whole mess or go put it back together. After I slept on it, I decided to go for it. It was going to take a lot of work and some thick skin. With the owner's permission, I began to put this place back in the black. With his approval, I hired private detectives to watch the store. Employees were helping themselves during the evening hours. Liquor, cigarettes, and beef were their favored items to steal. We next hired customers to come in and buy things. The employees were taking the customers money and then voiding the sales. It ended up in their pocket and not the register. The meat cutter was married to the bookkeeper. She always made the books look profitable, so there was no suspicion of the theft going on. This was only the beginning of my surveillance with one of his stores. I then started on the others. I was not popular, and I did not make any new friends. I was not fond of dishonest people and I really don't care what they thought of me. I knew where I came from and it gave me strength.

My boss was in his 20's, and he was on fire. He decided to open several family restaurants, a wholesale meat company, and a bag your own groceries store. This kind of grocery store had not been done in the area before. It was a fabulous new conception. My husband designed and built the counters for this innovative design.

I had no idea what I was getting myself into. This man's mind was like a hamster running on a spinning wheel, and he was running on it 24/7. I could barely keep up with him. We ended up moving into a brand-new state of the art office. I interviewed and hired staff to help us run it. I now had people helping me do all the bookkeeping and accounting. I was now orchestrating all the everyday operations. Office Manager was my new title. He had decided that he wanted to pursue his dream of becoming a pastor. He had started his training, and I had a lot more responsibility. One day he called me into his office, and he said he wanted to give me a raise. He told me to write down on a piece of paper what I thought my salary should be. He wrote down on a piece of paper what he thought I was worth. He told me to fold it up and pass it over to him. At the same time, he would pass his over to me. I can't remember exactly what I wrote on the piece of paper, but it was somewhere near maybe a dollar more than what I was getting. On his piece of paper, he gave me a $7.00 an hour increase in pay. Back in the 1970s that was a lot of money. I was making about $15 an hour. Considering I was making $4.25 per hour just a few months earlier this was quite an accomplishment. He also gave me his Lincoln Continental car to drive around while he was taking his classes.

As it turned out he had some money difficulties. The phenomenal rapid growth was not keeping up with the cash flow.

He had far more aspirations and expenses than he had dollars in his bank account. The bills were not getting paid. The first thing he stopped paying was his taxes. He was not paying his employee taxes and not paying the union dues. That wasn't even the worst of it. He had been opening checking accounts at different banks and transferring money back and forth. I didn't know it at the time, but that was illegal. The bank called me and asked me to come into the bank and help them reconcile his bank account with them. Now you must remember at this time in life there weren't any computers or Internet. Everything was done by hand. It did take a little while to reconcile it all. As it turned out, he owed the bank quite a bit of money. They had decided that I had more responsibility for money than he did. They made it mandatory that he could not write a check anymore unless I co-signed it. It was a lot of responsibility for a girl in her 20s. Not to mention that I had to manage all the employees, run the businesses, and keep track of him. He was really quite a nice guy, and I really did enjoy his company, but he kind of drove me crazy. I would do the tax returns, make the checks out to the IRS and to the state and the employees union for the taxes owed. I'd go into his office and ask him to sign them. I would co-sign them, and I put them on his desk to be mailed. Turns out he never did mail those checks. He had a million other ways to use the money. There was always something better to do with it.

My sense of loyalty and not giving up is in full swing.

CHAPTER 66

I Don't Want To Do This!

ONE DAY I GOT A telephone call from an attorney, and he asked me to come down and talk with him. I asked him what it was about, and he said it was about my job. I very innocently went to the attorney's office by myself to see what was going on. When I got there, I saw his wife with the attorney. They started asking me questions about bookkeeping. I answered all the questions as truthfully as possible. They asked me if I signed the checks for the taxes to be paid. I said that I did. They asked me what I had done with them after I signed them. I told them I would always put them on the desk of my boss to co-sign the checks and he said he would mail them. Our conversation was over, and I left. It turns out that his wife thought the reason he was having financial difficulties was my fault. She had hired this attorney to ask me all these questions to see if I could be liable for all the taxes that he didn't pay. All the union dues he didn't pay. Fortunately for me, I had told the truth and had done the job that I was supposed to be doing. I was not responsible for any of his financial shenanigans. A few months later it was self-evident that he had spent way more money than he had. The banks had all halted all his accounts from going back and forth with the transfers. He was forced to file for Chapter 13 bankruptcy. He quickly hired an attorney who specialized in bankruptcies. This attorney told me to save money that I needed to submit all this paperwork for the court. I also needed to comply with several things regarding filing for bankruptcy. I didn't know the first thing about bankruptcy. I was a young girl who didn't know how to do it. Let me tell you how quickly I learned. I basically filled out all the paperwork. I did all the worksheets and got all the information ready for the judge. I now hated my job. Now suddenly, I was in the middle of the biggest mess that I had nothing to do with. I was told by the judge that I could not quit my job until this bankruptcy was finalized. I was so upset I was riddled with anxiety. I hated all this pressure and responsibility that I was under. Then to top it all off, I had the complete responsibility for signing all the checks and budgeting the small amount of money that was now coming in. My boss was removed from his own bank accounts. I really liked him, he was a great guy with a lot of ambition and drive. I admired his determination and positive attitude. He always came up with a new solution to whatever problem was presented. I continued to work for him until it just didn't make any sense anymore. I had helped him through his bankruptcy, and now he could begin all over with a clean slate. He was kind to me, and I appreciated him. It was so much responsibility. Had I not had the upbringing that I had I would not be strong enough to go on this journey with him. It really showed me what strength and ability to survive I had learned as a young child. Even though it was challenging for me to go through those early times, I've always felt grateful for the lessons that I have learned from them. I never wanted anyone to ever feel sorry for me, and I was finally able to prove that those experiences were what helped me develop the character of perseverance, strength and sheer determination.

I thought about when I went over to one of the employee's homes to pick up some paperwork for my boss. She was the cook at one of the restaurants. She made the best pancakes there ever was. She wouldn't let anyone know the recipe. While I was at her house, her daughter stopped by. They both went into the kitchen and started cooking together. I remember they had their backs to me, and they were talking and cooking. I longingly was looking at them and thinking how amazing it was. I was so jealous at that moment of their loving relationship. It was beautiful, a mother and a daughter cooking in the kitchen together. I felt so sad when I left. I was so jealous that they were experiencing a beautiful, close mother-daughter moment. It was at that point I decided that I could possibly have a mother-daughter relationship of my own. Even though I didn't have a relationship with my mother, I could become a mother and have a relationship with my own child. I remember crying all the way home. I craved what they had. I realized that emotionally I was very empty. On the outside, I was confident and motivated. I had indeed numbed myself of my inner emotions for so long. I had spent most of my life taking care of others. I really did not know how to nurture myself.

CHAPTER 67

House Of Tom's Dreams

DURING THE TIME THAT I was working for my boss my personal life was growing by leaps and bounds as well. My friend that I had met at my previous job and I had become extremely close friends. Her husband hired Tom to work at his construction company while he was completing his carpentry apprenticeship. He was becoming a land developer as well as running his own construction business. He was looking for some cash to develop some property he had bought. I was quite a saver back then, and I happened to have $19,000 saved. Doesn't seem like a lot of money right now but at the time it seemed like a lot to me. I offered to loan it to him to help him develop some land that he was working on. He said he would need it for 30 days and at the end of 30 days he would pay me back plus $1,000 interest. At the end of the 30 days he asked me could he extend it for 60 days and I said sure. At the end of 60 days, he said he still was having a little bit of trouble coming up with the money and he offered me one of the parcels of land in exchange for the money I had loaned him. I said yes because I really did like the land and Tom was very excited at the prospect of having some property to build our own house on. He was selling the parcels for $40,000. The way I saw it I was doubling my money either way. We were just renting at the time. Tom decided he wanted to build our Dream House on the land. I agreed, and we started out making our house when we were in our early twenties. I had developed personal relationships with so many of the bankers that I had worked with from my previous job. There were several of them that were eager to offer a construction loan to build our house. They were so helpful to me they even would bring me draws on the credit to the office where I worked. I got a very fair interest rate and personalized service. We ended up borrowing about $80,000 from the construction loan. It was a beautiful custom three-story house with the best views of the mountains and the cook inlet. It was a beautiful home. After it was finished, we moved in, and I remember thinking this house needs a baby living here. I realized right then and there that my biological clock was ticking. I wanted a baby to complete this beautiful time in my life.

I actually cared enough to want something for myself.

CHAPTER 68

The Time Has Come

TOM HAD ALWAYS TOLD ME that he never wanted to have children. And to be honest, I really didn't think I wanted to have children either. I felt I had already raised my mother's children and that was quite enough for me. But suddenly with this big beautiful house it felt empty without children to me. After experiencing the longing, I had after watching the mother and daughter cooking in the kitchen I told him that I wanted to get pregnant. He said adamantly he did not want any children. I told him that's fine if you really don't want to have any children then you need to keep your penis in your pants. Well, he didn't keep it to himself. I was still working a lot of hours. When I went to buy some appliances for my new home the company that I bought them from was looking for some help in their office. I told them I could help them straighten things out on a part-time basis because I was still working full-time. I kept my other part-time jobs as well. I was busy all the time. I started to feel unable to do all my jobs because I was so sleepy. I would have to come home from work and take naps. I had quit all my little side jobs because I was so tired. I couldn't figure out what was going on. I usually had so much energy and required so little sleep. Lo and behold I was pregnant. I never got morning sickness, but I sure did get tired. I have to say that I absolutely loved being pregnant. When I told Tom the good news, he didn't talk to me for three days. He was not happy about it. After the initial shock, he finally started talking to me. The first thing he said was I'm not changing one dirty diaper, not one. He ended up changing every dirty diaper. I loved all the attention I got. I loved all the baby showers and lavish gifts. I loved it when I went to the grocery store, and they would carry my groceries out for me. I absolutely loved people taking care of me for the first time in my young life. It felt perfect. I liked it a lot. It made me feel very special. This was my time to experience unconditional love.

I started trying to wind down some of the work I had. I also started decorating the nursery in our new home. It was probably one of the most fun times I had experienced in my life so far. I was surrounded by so many beautiful, loving people in my life. I had baby shower, after baby shower. My friends were all so supportive of me, so happy for me. I can remember thinking that I never dreamed that this beautiful moment in my life would ever be a possibility. I also realized that because of my past I had been through the worst of things. I decided to give myself the most amazing future I could ever imagine. I could never have done the things in business at such an early age had I not been prepared for it early on in life. Taking care of a household and children is a tremendous task. It takes all kinds of hard work, talent, and determination. I learned how to handle people. I learned how to read people. I learned how to control myself in situations that were far beyond my years. I'm thankful for that. Lessons learned early paid off in the future.

CHAPTER 69

Not A Gerber Baby

EVEN THOUGH I WAS NOT due for 6 to 8 more weeks, I was totally prepared. I had talked to a psychic that had told me the baby was coming early. We were having a fantastic prime rib dinner at my best friend's house when suddenly my water broke. It was six weeks earlier than my delivery date. I went home and called the doctor's emergency number. It was already about 10:30 at night. I told him my water had broken and he said to go to the hospital immediately. Tom said I should just go to sleep and I probably would feel better in the morning. Are you kidding me? I told him no, we need to go to the hospital. When I got to the hospital, I was already dilated 5 centimeters. I had the baby five hours after I had broken my water. I never used any drugs for my delivery. I did it entirely naturally. It really wasn't that hard considering she only weighed 5 lbs. 9 oz. I'll never forget my pediatrician coming into my room that morning at the hospital and saying "I have good news for you and bad news. The good news is you have a beautiful baby girl. The bad news is she's not a Gerber baby." Her Apgar score was very low. She was a preemie. That usually comes with medical complications. She started giving me a run for my money right away.

She was born with jaundice. She had to have her blood checked every two hours. She was put in an incubator with special lights on her. She was not interested in eating anything. She was placed in ICU right after she was delivered. She had to stay there for five more weeks. She had lost so much of her original weight. Her weight had plummeted to four pounds. She was so tiny, and they put a black blindfold on her. This was so the lights could burn out jaundice and not damage her eyes. We called her the Frito Bandito because she was a yellow color. She was the size of a little tiny, baby piece of roast that would fir in the palm of my hand.

It was the saddest day for me when it was time for me to check out of the hospital, without my baby. She was still too sick to leave the hospital. I remember thinking that it was like ordering a new car, It arrives. It needs a little work to be perfect, so you can't drive it home. I was so sad, but I knew it was the best thing for her.

Instead of dwelling on my sad feelings I went straight back to work and caught up on the things I had not been able to do while in the hospital.

Her jaundice had gotten much worse. She needed a complete blood transfusion. Fortunately, I was able to provide the blood for the procedure. Tom went in with her while they gave her the blood. I waited in the waiting room. My comfort level for hospitals was very compromised at this point.

While I sat waiting for this to be over with a friend of mine Joe and his girlfriend Angel just happened to stop by to be with me in the waiting room. This was quite a surprise to me as I had not spoken to anyone about being there. He had given me a prediction that I was going to become pregnant and that it would be a preemie. He said that he felt that I needed support and they did not want me to be alone. So they took a chance that I was at the hospital. I really appreciated the comfort and support. I have never been very good about asking for help or support. I was used to being the strong one. It felt really good but I was guarded and did not let my emotions show. I always held everything in and never wanted to appear weak.

The transfusion was complete and they felt it had flushed out most of the bilirubin that had ravaged her tiny body. They put her back under the lights in the incubator. She finally started to gain weight. I pumped my breast milk and they fed it to her in the tiniest little baby bottle. She had plummeted to only four pounds. Her pediatrician felt that being in our home would help her thrive. As

soon as she reached five pounds he agreed to let me take her home.
I was so grateful and excited to finally begin my new journey......
motherhood. I wanted to be a perfect mother. Tom was so good
about always staying in the hospital with her every day while I stayed
at home and worked. The first time that she had a bowel movement
he changed her diapers. I knew then that it was all going to be okay.
I finally brought the baby home. She was dressed in a dolls dress
because of her tiny size. No one really prepares you for what it's going
to be like to have a baby. I just thought I was going to have this
incredible loving feeling towards this new child. It really didn't feel
like that. I thought there must be something wrong with me. I mean,
I really liked having her, and I was excited to have this baby. But there
just wasn't this incredible love exuding from my being that I thought
there would be. I thought I was going to have Golden Angels come
down and trumpets blaring, and fairy dust being dripped all over me.
I was waiting for this fantastic love experience. It did not come. The
only emotion I felt was sadness. I sat outside on the cold deck, and it
was about 10 degrees. I was crying and just wondering what the heck
was wrong with me. Why did everyone else have this beautiful, loving
feeling towards babies? To me, it just felt average. I can remember
thinking to myself did I just make the biggest mistake of my life. I
really felt confused, but I was afraid to tell anybody how I really felt.

CHAPTER 70

I Got This

IT WAS TIME FOR HER first trip to the doctors, and I got the diaper bag ready. I went out in the below-freezing weather. I started the car engine heater. I bathed her, put on a snowsuit and wrapped her in blankets. I put her in the car seat. Strapped her in, grabbed the diaper bag and started the car. Off I went on my first visit to the pediatrician. I was so proud of myself. I had prepared the most fantastic diaper bag with extra clothes, blankets, and diaper cream. Everything that you could imagine was in that bag. I was quite sure I could possibly become the mother of the year just by the diaper bag alone. The nurse put us in our room to wait for the doctor. She decided it was time to go to the bathroom in her diaper. The doctor walked in right at the same time. I was so embarrassed. This was the first time I was no longer in control. I apologized to the doctor and went straight to work and began to take care of that dirty diaper. Since she was a preemie, she had to have little tiny diapers. The doctor asked me if I had a clean diaper to put on her? I pulled out my fabulous diaper bag with everything in the world in this bag except …. diapers. There goes my mother of the year award. He didn't have any preemie diapers, so we had to kind of jerry-rig a regular baby diaper to fit. I was so embarrassed that when I got out of his office and to my car, I just started crying and I thought I don't know if I can do this. This is so crazy. I felt that I was so confident and able to achieve things because I was so strong. This little tiny baby literally brought me to my knees. It was a lot harder than I thought it would be. She cried a lot. She had colic. She slept in our room because I was so afraid that she would stop breathing. What if I didn't hear her. My mental state at the time was fragile. I was still working full time. I rarely got much rest. Nursing kept me from getting an entire night's sleep. This really was an entirely different scenario than I had envisioned. Where was that sweet baby that you see pictures of in the lullaby books?

On my next trip to the pediatrician, I told him that she didn't sleep very much. She never slept through the night. She cried a lot. I wasn't sure if I was doing something wrong. He assured me that I wasn't. He told me to give her a little bit of mint on her tongue, and that would probably stop the colic. She would start to sleep through the night eventually. I put her down and about 2 a.m. she woke up with her usual crying and I was sleepy. Through my sleepy haze, I remembered the doctor had told me about using the mint. I went into my pantry and got a bottle of mint extract and opened it up. I was so tired I wasn't really thinking clearly. I just put a drop on her tongue, I thought. It turned out that it was very concentrated. She started foaming at the mouth. She was crying louder and harder than ever before. I thought I had killed her for sure. Did I deserve this precious gift? I found myself in tears questioning my abilities. After she lived through that, I decided that she was a lot tougher than I was. I probably could make it as a mom. I remember the next time that I put her to sleep in her cradle by herself it was Christmas Eve. When I woke up Christmas Day, I realized I had slept through the night. I ran to the Cradle because I thought for sure she was dead. She had stopped breathing, and I had slept through it, I thought. What kind of Christmas was this going to be? She wasn't dead at all, she had just slept through the night. What a relief. Even though I had been through all of this with my siblings, it was entirely different with my own child. Having your very own child changes everything. I would say that having a child taught me all about flexibility. Up to that point, I had a schedule, and I planned every minute of my day. I used all sixty seconds wisely. All of them! I never wasted a minute. From now on my time was not my own. It was my job to now become flexible. Not a word I was used to.

It was very important to Tom that she be baptized in the Catholic church. His two sisters joined us for this blessed event. Right after Christmas, we went to get her christened. I bought her the most beautiful christening gown. Off to church we went, it was so cute. It was a very fulfilling and magical experience. We came home for lunch after her christening. I put her in her cradle for a sweet little nap in her beautiful white christening gown. We were all so tired after our meal that we all took short naps. I awoke to the worst smelling odor I had ever smelled. I followed my nose to where it was coming from. It led me straight to the baby. I went over and checked on her, and she had gone to the bathroom, and it was so abundant. Her beautiful white christening gown was now brown. I could not believe she would even think of soiling this beautiful hand-smocked dress. You see what I mean? My thoughts were foggy, and I was delusional.

CHAPTER 71

Control

THE WAY I STARTED TO live my life after leaving my mother's house was to always be in control of everything. No surprises. Every aspect of my life was planned. There was never any chaos or violence. Everything was in its place. Every minute used wisely.

I sort of felt like that was a turning point for me. My life was never going to be perfect again. I was no longer in control. My dilemma was how do I find a balance. I figured out that those days were in my past. Everything was going to be different now. I stopped wearing clothes that needed to be dry cleaned. I stayed in my jammies until I left the house. That way when I got thrown up on, I could just change quickly. I realized that I had a weak stomach. I do not like any fluids coming out of any orifices. Drooling, throw up, poop, snot and any kind of gooey stuff was not my friend. I started buying clothes that could be thrown into a washer and dryer. Showers were now a luxury. Baths were unheard of. I started looking for an adult size bib.

I must admit that Tom enjoyed having the baby very much. I was surprised since he didn't want to have any children. He was the first one to change her dirty diapers, and he changed most of them. It just didn't work out for me to be changing those nasty dirty diapers. I didn't like it. I did not want to do it. It did not seem to bother him at all. He really loves babies. It was not my favorite, and I hated carrying around that diaper bag. Just the thought of forgetting something haunted me. Don't get me wrong there were things I liked about her. Mostly they had to do with shopping for items for her though. I felt so shallow.

During these times Ronny would always pop into my mind. I would wonder about his children and hope that he was a good dad and that he was happy.

CHAPTER 72

I Made It

HER FIRST BIRTHDAY WAS QUICKLY approaching. I can so vividly remember that in my mind it was more about my survival and it was a celebration for me. I know that sounds bad. A year had gone by, and she was still alive. I felt I deserved a party for myself. I decided to go to Southern California to celebrate it with my and Tom's family. We had her first birthday celebration at Tom's sister's house. She made the most amazing huge chocolate cake that was in the shape of a big bear. And it had about a hundred little tiny candy bars on the base of where the bear sat. I had bought her the cutest small pair of blue overalls. I set individual rhinestones and sewed lace and appliques all over them. I put her name in rhinestones. That was her first birthday outfit, and she was barefoot. In my opinion, she looked adorable! I had never fed her anything to eat with sugar in it. She got her first piece of sweet cake on her first birthday. She puckered up her face. Licked her fingers and then decided she liked it.

I was so over the top being healthy with feeding this beautiful baby. I soaked almonds overnight to make almond milk for her. I made my own baby food. I never used a single instant anything. I mashed a few organic steamed vegetables. I also had a yogurt maker, and I made it fresh daily. I used to make her yogurt with avocados and wheat germ. I kept the house empty of packaged processed products and sugary sweets. I absolutely loved making healthy food for her. I also devoured every book I could find on how to be the perfect mother. I read dr. Spock and every other baby-raising book that I could find. I took her to Mommy and Me gym classes. We did exercises together. I took her to swimming lessons. She learned how to hold her breath underwater. This was all before she was 6 months old. I read to her several times a day. She really liked books. She was such a good baby. She was quite a lazy baby. I can remember the nurse in the ICU saying she had never seen anything like it. She would not even hold her own bottle. I had several friends who were having babies around the same time, and we would get all our babies together. They were all crawling and walking and being very social. My daughter would just sit there in my lap. She was quiet, she didn't walk when all the others were walking. My baby didn't cry much after she got over the colic. She indeed didn't crawl on furniture. I gave her pacifiers, stuffed toys, and blankets for comfort. She spits out the pacifier, ignores the stuffies and pees on the blankets. She did not want any of those things to comfort her. On one trip to the pediatrician, I said that I was a little worried because she was 15 months old and she hadn't even started to walk yet. All my friend's babies were already walking at 6-7 months. He assured me that if she walked to kindergarten, everything would be fine. Then one day she just got up and walked all around the house. There was no practicing involved. She just got up and walked. I wondered to myself, had she been practicing at night while I was asleep? As it turns out that's just kind of how she did things for the rest of her life. She would observe until she felt completely confident and then get up and do it. I breathed a huge sigh of relief when I realized my daughter would also be walking into kindergarten with all the other kindergarteners. I just needed patience, lots of patience.

Remind yourself
That you cannot fail
At being yourself

CHAPTER 73

Stay At Home Mom

I HAD DECIDED TO SELL Tupperware full time and quit all my other jobs. I could stay home with my daughter all day. My husband could stay home with her at night when I would go out and do my parties. It was easy for me to sell the product because I personally loved it. I had been recruited by a manager who I had met while having a party at my home. We became fast friends. She shared with me that she wanted to be the number one manager in our region. She told me I could help her get there. I loved a good challenge, and I really cared about helping her become the best she could be. We had the best promotional speakers to come to visit us and give us motivational talks. I held on to every word they said. I learned how to sell, and I was good at it. I loved the fellowship of working with a team. I loved selling. I loved winning all the prizes and trips. The money was amazing and I got a new car every year. She became # 1 in the region and was celebrated in front of everyone at a big convention! I was so proud of her. By working so hard with her, I became # 2 in our dealership. I also won a coveted spot in our region. One time one of the regionals came to visit our dealership. He asked me to do a talk for the other managers. The subject was about why I became so successful so quickly. I pondered that for a very long time. We all have the same opportunities and tools to work with. The only explanation I could come up with was that I just did it. I did not procrastinate.

I got up every day and went to work. I felt that work came easily to me because of my childhood. Early on it became clear to me that I had the responsibilities of an entire family. If I didn't do it, it really would have been a disaster. I also shared my secret of using all sixty seconds of every minute wisely. I also really enjoyed all the recognition and gifts. It was so exciting to be in the spotlight and be rewarded for my accomplishments.

It helped me realize that I was born with a beautiful soul and spirit as we all are. I believed in myself. I suppose I unknowingly loved myself. I had to accept it. If I had not, I would have turned out like the other people that were living around me when I was a child. God honestly gave me a unique light inside of me, and I was determined to keep it burning.

I believed in treating others as I wanted to be treated myself. That became my motto. I wanted to give to all that needed it.

get on your knees and pray, then get on your feet and work.

CHAPTER 74

It's Time

I WAS READY TO MAKE a change. After all, I was the girl who used to move about every two months, and I had already lived in Alaska for ten years. We were getting ready to take a road trip. We kept a car in Oregon at my brother-in-law's house so that when we flew out of Alaska, we would have our own car. We flew into Oregon and hopped in the car. We started driving down the Freeway. I remembered looking on the side of the road off the 5 freeway. We had gotten to Northern California. I saw some fantastic cute houses in the distance, and I asked Tom to pull over. Let's go look at them, I squealed. He agreed to pull over, and we went and walked through them. I loved them, and I put down a deposit on one of them right then and there. When we got back home to Alaska, I put my house up for sale, and it sold in 24 hours. I took it as a sign from God that he was letting me out of Alaska. I wanted to live back in California. Tom was not that excited to move. I sure was ready to go.

Once again, we packed all our belongings, and we headed off to Sacramento. My new home. I did not know a single person in Sacramento. It did not deter me though.

CHAPTER 75

Uh Oh

I WENT TO VISIT MY very best friend Pam for the last time before I would be leaving Alaska. I would be getting on a plane that evening for California. We had dinner. My daughter said she wasn't feeling good and I told her to take a little nap before we got on the plane. She woke up a couple of hours later throwing up, and her temperature was high. I rushed her to the hospital. The pediatrician came out of the emergency room saying once again, I have good news and bad news. The good news is that she's going to be okay, and I can take her on the plane to Sacramento. The bad news is he thought she had a serious urinary tract infection. He instructed me to see a urologist as soon as I got to Sacramento. He gave me some antibiotics for her. I never even missed my plane that night.

This began a very long journey for us. Once again, Tom met us at the airport in Sacramento. He had come early and found us a place to live. I shared my concerns about our daughter. We started searching immediately for a urologist. After many trips to various doctors and several tests, we learned that she had not developed her ureter tubes. Without those, her urine stayed in her kidneys and damaged them. I went to so many different doctors trying to find a urologist that I could relate to. I didn't know anyone in town. I didn't really know anyone that could refer me to a good doctor. I finally heard about a doctor that lived in Los Angeles. They had a children's hospital there that he worked out of. They specialized in treating little ones. They used small needles and had a fun waiting room. Tom had bought her a little stuffed dog to always take with her to the doctors. She named him Brownie. At 3 years old she finally bonded with something. The doctor would take x-rays of Brownie before her. Basically, brownie the little-stuffed dog was poked with needles and had his own x-rays. Every treatment she was getting, Brownie got first. He even had his own chart at the hospital. Tom got brownie his own collar and pet I.D. tag. Once we had established a rapport with a great doctor, we were ready to proceed. She needed surgery.

We had bought a new house with the money from the other home we sold. We did not have jobs yet. Our daughter needed surgery. We met with the hospital. They informed us that we needed 30,000.00 cash to admit her. We did not have insurance. That did not include the doctor or anesthesiologist. We sold our new home. I remember thinking how blessed I was that we owned a house that we could sell to get that money. We worked out payment plans with everyone else. Off to surgery we go. It was supposed to be a surgery that was about two hours long. After 5 hours we were still waiting for the doctor to come out and talk to us. I asked the receptionist what was going on. She did not know. I decided I would go into the operating room and find out for myself. As you can imagine, I was stopped immediately, and someone came out to talk to us. All was well. It was just a lot more work once we had gotten inside than he could see on the x-rays. Relief consumed me.

I held back the tears raised my chin up and carried on.

DEAR GOD, I WANNA TAKE A MINUTE, NOT TO ASK FOR ANYTHING FROM YOU, BUT SIMPLY TO SAY THANK YOU, FOR ALL I HAVE.

CHAPTER 76

On Our Own

THIS WHOLE SURGERY AND HAVING to move again was hard on Tom. He wanted to go back to Alaska. He went to live with his best friend. I wished him well, and I carried on. My daughter healed slowly. I started to look for employment. I had begun selling Tupperware after I had my baby in Alaska. I became a manager in a short amount of time. A Tupperware station wagon was one of my perks. I went and checked into the Sacramento dealership. They welcomed me and promptly gave me a station wagon. I started cold calling in the neighborhood. The office would send me leads too. I met the most helpful people. Friendships were formed in no time at all. I felt entirely at home. I got lucky and got in with a great group of customers too. I was making a comfortable living. We were living in an farmland area. I would visit the farm every few days and bring home whatever they were growing and was in season at the time. I fixed a lot of corn on the cob. The tomatoes were so great too. There is nothing like eating farm-fresh food. It tastes so alive!

My daughter's check-ups were not what I would have liked. Everything with this child was never easy. She needed more surgery. Tom was still in Alaska. I had to deal with all of this by myself. I got the surgery scheduled and asked Tom to come back for her appointment. He came back and went with me to the hospital. Everything went well. She was so brave. I hated her going under the anesthesia. We tried to make it a positive experience. My sister and brother came to visit. None of Tom's family came to the hospital. I felt so sorry for all her medical experiences. For the next 5 years, it was back and forth to the hospital. In and out of surgeries.

Promote what you love instead of bashing what you hate.

CHAPTER 77

A Chance Encounter

WHILE AT A TUPPERWARE PARTY I was giving, my hostess and I formed a friendship. Soon after I went to a craft show. I was introduced to rubber stamps. I bought 3 of them and a stamp pad. I began stamping everything in sight. The search was on! Where could I get more of these beautiful things? I found out that I could buy them wholesale if I purchased two of the same images. I started asking my friends if they would want to buy some. They did. One of the guests at a party worked for the state. She started selling them at her work for me, and I would give her free stamps. The next thing I knew I had people coming to my house to buy stamps. My former hostess friend said she had a friend in Los Angeles. She was interested in opening a retail store. She was looking for a partner. She thought we would be perfect together. Her family owned some retail property. Things seemed to all be lining up for this to happen. We started a cute little shop. We carried educational books for children and educational toys. Rubber stamps and stationery were my primary focus. The first day we opened, we sold $400.00. Amazing! We added gifts that could be personalized too.

I researched other stores to see how they were doing things. I found a charming store in Southern California. I called the owner, and I asked her if I could pay her for a consultation. She agreed, and I paid her $250.00. We soon became terrific friends.

We started going to wholesale gift shows together. We exchanged ideas and sources for our merchandise. It was a long-distance business relationship that turned into a friendship. We started talking on the phone daily. It was so nice to have a friend with the same things in common.

My daughter still needed medical attention. When we would go to the doctor appointments in Los Angeles we would always make plans to see her. We would usually with her. She would come to Sacramento to visit us and spend the night too. She became a big part of my daughter's life. She was kind, generous and great with kids. She was creative and talented. She told everyone that I paid her to be my friend! We even started staying at each other's homes. It was a beautiful friendship. We would always call each other and be supportive. We also went out of state together to go on buying trips. Good Times! My store was doing quite well. I decided it was time to expand. Tom & I started searching for another location. We found a great space. It was in a brand-new strip mall. Tom had built our first store and did a fabulous job. He agreed to do our second one. He had an empty space that had never been used. It was so fun to design it and watch it come to fruition. It was everything. I loved it. I was so excited to have such a great store. I had a classroom in the back of the store. I started teaching classes. The one thing I learned about having two locations. It takes twice as much of your time. You don't make twice as much money. You pay twice as many employees. We decided to sell our first location. My partner wanted out of our relationship. It was hard having a long-distance partner. She told us an amount of money that she wanted for her percentage. We bought her out. It did put a drain on our bank account.

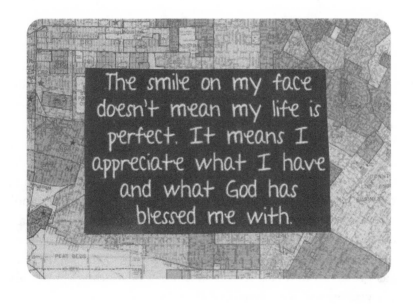

The smile on my face doesn't mean my life is perfect. It means I appreciate what I have and what God has blessed me with.

CHAPTER 78

Wanderlust

TOM WANTED TO MAKE ANOTHER trek to Alaska for the summer. He decided to take our daughter on the journey. She was now six years old. Her health was stable. I agreed, and they were off on an Alaskan adventure. I managed the store. I really enjoyed being alone. I was able to devote a lot more time to my work. I started closing the store one day a week so I could have a little time for myself. I joined a club with a pool. I started swimming and tanning. I was in heaven. One day when I got out of the club pool, I went inside to take a shower. Someone had shampooed their hair. There was soap all over the floor. I slipped on it and broke my foot. I was in a cast for months. I was so sad. My pool days were over. It was great timing because the summer was winding down. My family was on their way home.

My daughter was beginning kindergarten. We had enrolled her in a private school. She thrived in this beautiful environment. It suited her very well. Every aspect of our life seemed to be right where it was supposed to be. The school she attended was the Waldorf School.

CHAPTER 79

Willow

SHE MET A NEW FRIEND there named Willow. They spent every day with each other. Willow's mom was a single parent going to school and struggling financially. We embraced Willow as if she was our own daughter. What a joy she was to have around. On the weekends the two would reenact stories they had read. Carly loved Annie Oakley. She even had a part in one of the community plays featuring Annie Oakley. On Saturday mornings they would begin their day making a stagecoach in the living room. I gave them journals. They drew all the items that they would buy at a general store. They set up a small store. They designed the clothing they would need for their journey. They wrote a diary of their daily adventures.

Willow's mom was single and going to school herself. Willow spent many days and nights with our family. The neighbors used to ask me if I got child support for her. She was such a pleasure to be with. The creativity between my daughter and her just flowed. I loved her like my own child. We are still in touch.

CHAPTER 80

Creativity

WHILE WATCHING ALL OF THE beautiful things Willow and my daughter created was when I started to realize the many talents she shared with my mother. She started sewing classes. She drew very well for her age. When we would take our annual trips to San Francisco, she wanted to go straight to Neiman Marcus. She wanted to see all the couture clothing. Her sketchpad would come out, and she would begin to draw her own designs. She was 6 years old.

I kept her supplied in the best art supplies that were available. She also loved to read. All of us liked to read. There were always lots of books around the house. Lots of art supplies everywhere, and we all loved using them. I was fortunate that I could be creative, do what I liked, and the money followed me.

CHAPTER 81

Time to Travel

WHEN MY DAUGHTER TURNED 10 years old, we were married for 20 years, and my husband was 40, we decided to take a new adventure. My husband thought it was a good idea to sell most everything we owned. We sold our stores. I applied to her school to do homeschooling. He converted our van into a mini motorhome. We rented a 10x10 storage unit. We sold everything except what would fit in this storage including my car. He allowed us each one storage bin of our belongings that we could bring with us on our trip. We then headed off for a journey across the USA and Canada. We took off from Sacramento for a year-long adventure. Yes, we were off to see the USA in our Chevrolet. We agreed to spend less than $100.00 per day. That included: gas, housing, food and drink, and any supplies we might need. There were several ways we discovered to save money. We needed to keep on our financial goal to see everything we wanted to see. We left April 1, 1991, for our adventure. It was a risky thing to do. Some called us foolish. We had heard that before when we left California for Alaska. When we left Alaska for California the same sentiments were expressed. How could we leave our successful business and sell all of our belongings to go travel? All of those events changed our lives for sure. I have no regrets and I am so happy Tom encouraged these events to happen. I was born to make my life worth living. Up to this point, I have lived every minute to the fullest. These journeys have created my story so far.

EPILOGUE

HERE IS WHERE I SAY goodbye for now. It is not the end. It is just the beginning of my next level of life. I hope that you are intrigued enough to want to read more. I represent who we all can be. We just need to say to ourselves I am…fill in the blanks. Our thoughts become things so always think highly of yourself.

RANDOM THOUGHTS

Most importantly just do it. Do not wait for the right time. Be the right time. Follow your inner being and manifest all of your possibilities. Do not listen to people when they say negative things to and about you. It has been my experience that they are merely telling you how they feel about themselves. They really have nothing to do with you. It is their own business, not yours. Just as they do not know inside your mind, you cannot possibly know what is inside of theirs. Do not ever let anyone take your joy away. Remember this is your life and your time. Are you going to use wisely every sixty seconds in the minutes that just past? I know for sure I did. I am proud of who I have become. I am not perfect. I embrace my strength and the ability to help others. I hope that you find strength in my words. It has been my experience that my best assets were also my worst assets. It was up to me how I used them.

This is my story!

AFTERWORD

I really encourage you to email me at missvickyb@gmail.com.

I can't wait to share with you my two-year journey of traveling around the USA. Here is a snippet of things to come. This is the part of my story where I share with you how I touched and was touched by each person I met. It is the story of how I began to get in touch with my spiritual guide. I was able to develop it and listen to what my gifts were and how to use them.

We left Sacramento and headed towards Idaho. We went to see my husband's very best friend! When we got there, we were surprised to see him looking sort of gray. My sense told me there was something wrong with him physically. My husband talked him into going to see the doctor. He said he felt he had been running at about 60%. He went the next morning and found out his body was raging with Leukemia. This was such a shock to hear. He was 40 years old, just paid off all his business expenses, the favorite dentist just adopted 2 kids, and his life seemed to be up and running. I strongly felt this was the reason we had come here at this time. He started treatment immediately. One year later he was gone. He died on April Fool's Day. He was so funny and had such a great personality. It was a massive loss to everyone. I knew at that moment why we had taken this trip. I understood why we went to see him first. Even though it was too late to save him, he did get a year to take care of his business. He lived the last year knowing he was going to die. He did exactly what he wanted every day. In some small way, it was a gift. Not the one we would have wanted, but a gift just the same.

I kept a travel diary so I could remember everywhere we went. The budget was held daily. If we did not drink anything but water. We stayed in a lot of campgrounds. Bought most of our meal ingredients at the local farmer's market. We also ate at as many culinary schools as possible. The food was delicious and inexpensive. We usually ate two meals a day. We stayed remarkably healthy, and we never got sick.

My third book is about when I became a millionaire. It is quite a story. It was such a surprise to me. This book is about the chain of events that showed me the American Dream. Here is a taste of things to come.

Our lives had changed forever after our statewide journey. We found a place to rent and began to put our life in touch with our new direction.

My daughter went back to school. I had to think about what I was going to do next to earn money. I wanted to do something different that I had not done before. On our trip, I visited lots of businesses. I saw one that I thought I might be interested in. I did not want to copy them.

Someone may copy you; I have been copied many times. In my soul and mind I can come up with so many new things. No one can keep up with what is in my head and heart and hands. Because they have not walked in my shoes. Copying is the best form of flattery they say. I personally got tired of all the flattery. Show me the money and I will take my flattery to the bank. People copy people, that's what they do. It has no criteria; they copy what they see. The truth is everyone remembers the first time they saw the original. I strived to be original.

In closing, I want to add some personal thoughts that I often think about. I hope now you will think of them too. Add your thoughts of what has made your life worth living to mine.

I thank Eric Clapton every day for loving the blues. He is the one for me that opened eyes to the soul and music of black musicians in America. A white man from over the pond. He could not believe the treasures he found in the Blues and shared it with anyone who would listen.

I thank GOD every day for placing me in the ghetto right alongside other people with the same struggles I had. Many times, in my life I have been the minority. The struggle is real.

The one thing I have learned is this: The only true sin is judgment. It is talked about in the bible. As a young girl sitting in my Baptist church, I heard the Black pastor telling the stories of the bible. I heard them. I decided at ten years old not to judge people. We all can learn from that. Don't judge, love! Love and be accepting of what we do not always know about.

I remember hearing Charles Barkley say this: People that don't like black people do not know them. I found that to be so poetic and true. Not just black people but all people.

I personally thank L.B. Poly High School for the gift of integration. I lived across the street and was thankful to be in that neighborhood. I made a lot of friends there. I learned so much about all kinds of people and their cultures. It truly formed my personality. I met all three boyfriends I ever had there. I still love each one of them. I am still friends with my fellow Jack Rabbits and feel that they will always be my true friends. They knew my story and accepted me for who I was. They have watched my story grow and to this day continue to cheer me on. I appreciate that and always love hearing their stories.

I would love to hear about your story too! So please email me and follow me on Facebook: Vicky Bratsakis Breslin.

Facebook: Miss Vicky says just do it
ETSY: http//www.etsy.com/yourshops/shops/MissVickySays
missvickyb@gmail.com

MissVickySays
You can't wait until life isn't hard anymore to be happy.

YOUR TIME IS LIMITED,
SO DON'T WASTE IT LIVING SOMEONE ELSE'S LIFE.
DON'T BE TRAPPED BY DOGMA
WHICH IS LIVING WITH THE RESULTS OF OTHER PEOPLE'S THINKING.
DON'T LET THE NOISE OF
OTHERS' OPINIONS DROWN
OUT YOUR OWN INNER VOICE.
AND MOST IMPORTANT, HAVE THE COURAGE
TO FOLLOW YOUR HEART AND INTUITION,
THEY SOMEHOW ALREADY KNOW WHAT
YOU TRULY WANT TO BECOME.
EVERYTHING ELSE
IS SECONDARY.
—STEVE JOBS, 2005

ACKNOWLEDGMENTS

I WOULD LIKE TO ACKNOWLEDGE the people, places, and things that made this story possible.

Thank you all for your contribution to this life that I have led.

My Creator, parents, siblings, family, friends and all the folks I have met along the way. All the places I have journeyed to that have helped me realize how much there is to discover.

The things that I have gone through good, bad, interesting, exciting, painful, or ugly. The things that have shaped my life.

Day by day another page would be written. Sometimes hour by hour, minute by minute and even by the second. These things all contributed to my story.

I would like to give thanks to two friends that really encouraged me to write this story; Both really thought I had something to share. It is my pleasure to share the story of my life.

Thank you, Scott and Beverly. Here is the story. It is my hope that you learn something new about me.